Reality and Mysticism

Utkal Studies in Philosophy – IV

General Editor: P. K. Mohapatra

REALITY AND MYSTICISM

— PERSPECTIVES IN THE UPANIṢADS —

by

R. Puligandla

Published by
D.K. Printworld (P) Ltd., New Delhi

in association with
Department of Special Assistance in Philosophy
Utkal University, Bhubaneswar

Cataloging in Publication Data—DK
Courtesy: D.K. Agencies (P) Ltd. <docinfo@dkagencies.com>

Puligandla, R., 1930-2022 author.
Reality and mysticism : perspectives in the Upaniṣads / by R. Puligandla.
pages cm. – (Utkal studies in philosophy ; IV)
Reprint. Originally published: 1997.
Includes bibliographical references.

1. Upanishads – Criticism, interpretation, etc. 2. Mysticism – Hinduism. I. Utkal University. Department of Special Assistance in Philosophy, issuing body, publisher. II. Title. III. Series: Utkal studies in philosophy ; IV.

BL1124.57.P85 2017 DDC 294.59218 23

ISBN 978-81-246-0092-4

First Published in India in 1997
Second impression, 2017; Third impression, 2025
Author: Ramakrishna Puligandla 1930-2022

Printed and published by :
D.K. Printworld (P) Ltd.
Regd. office : Vedaśrī, F-395, Sudarshan Park
ESI Metro Station, New Delhi - 110 015
Phones : (011) 4172 2626, 98713 94815
e-mail : indology@dkprintworld.com
Web : www.dkprintworld.com

in association with:
Department of Special Assistance in Philosophy
Utkal University
Bhubaneswar (Orissa)

Preface

EVER since the Department of Philosophy at Utkal came under the UGC programme of Special Assistance, a series of publications under the title "Utkal Studies in Philosophy" are being brought out periodically. *Reality and Mysticism* constitutes the fourth volume of books published under this series. The contents of the present volume comprise of the learned ideas of Professor Ramakrishna Puligandla of the University of Toledo, U.S.A., who delivered three illuminating lectures during his stay here in 1996 as a Visiting Professor under the DSA programme.

'Mysticism' as a concept often used in philosophical discussions, has been the subject of hairsplitting controversy among philosophers and even an object of embarrassment to philosophical discourse. Generally mysticism has been thought to be antithetical to logical thinking which dominantly characterises philosophical thinking. Western writers, in general, consider mysticism as illogical, irrational and even non-moral. In this vein, Western critics have often been inclined to brand Indian philosophy as mystical, meaning thereby that Indian philosophy virtually contains no logic. Some even have gone on record as saying that there is no philosophy in India. In bold contrast, Professor Puligandla takes up a contrary view defending mysticism as a virtue rather than a limitation of Indian philosophy. In admitting that the dominant trends in Indian philosophy, like that of the Upaniṣads as well as of Saṁkara and Nāgārjuna, lie in mystical understanding of the Reality, Puligandla claims that this mysticism is not illogical or irrational, but is meant to awaken and inspire one's mind for the quest of the ultimate reality, the one non-dual *Brahman*. It consists in the transcendence of all categorial knowledge, all forms of conceptual-perceptual ratiocination. It is, in this sense "cognitive mysticism" (courtesy B.K. Matilal), which is philosophically attractive and intellectually stimulating. Thus understood, the Indian brand of mysticism is far from being illogical or irrational, much less non-moral as alleged by western critics.

Puligandla's interpretation of mysticism is stoutly bold, intellectually stimulating and revealingly original. The book will certainly raise controversy but is sure to throw fresh light on mysticism as it is related to knowledge, truth and reality. Scholars and researchers in philosophy will have rewarding results from reading the book.

I thank the author for being with us and enriching our research programme as evidenced in this book.

I thank my fellow editors for their useful help in bringing out the volume. The UGC deserve our thanks and gratitude for providing fund for the publication of this volume under the Special Assistance Programme.

April 20, 1997

P. K. Mohapatra
Professor & Coordinator, D.S.A.
Department of Philosophy
Utkal University

Contents

Introduction

The Upaniṣadic literature marks the turning point in the philosophical and cultural history of India. Though considered an integral part of the Vedas, the contents of the Upaniṣads are totally different from the other segments of the Vedas, viz., *saṁhitās*, *brāhmaṇas* and *āraṇyakas*, since the path suggested in the Upaniṣads is that of *jñānamārga* as opposed to the *karma-mārga* of the rest of the Vedic literature. The Upaniṣadic passages are sometimes terse and cryptic and quite often the presentations are non-systematic. However they are philosophically fertile and quite elevating in their spirit. The dominant metaphysical trend of the Upaniṣads points towards man's quest for the realisation of the ultimate truth. The metaphysical quest expressed in rudimentary form in some Vedic hymns like *Nāsadīya sūkta* and *Hiraṇyagarbha sūkta* finds its final fulfillment in the realisation that the one and non-dual *Brahman* is the ultimate reality and the *ātman* is non-different from the *Brahman*. The Upaniṣadic seers not content with the relative nature of the finite and empirical proclaim: *nālpe sukamasti, bhūmaive sukham, yo vai bhūma tat sukham* (the bliss is not to be found in the finite, that which alone is infinite and all-embracing is the ground of blissfulness).[1]

At the same time, the Upaniṣads insist that the *Brahman* is

---

1. *Chhāndogya Upaniṣad*, VII. 23.1.

ineffable, It transcends the conceptual and linguistic framework, It is beyond names and forms: *yato vāco nivartante aprāpya manasā saḥ.*[2]

The categorial framework is meant for the cognition of anything that is phenomenal and empirical. This Upaniṣadic trend has its ramifications in most of the philosophical systems in India, including even the unorthodox schools of thought like Buddhism.

The style, presentation and the dominant metaphysical trend of the Upaniṣads are unique in many respects. For many they represent the genuine expressions of the spiritual experience, while for others they are rhapsodies on mysticism; for others they present highest metaphysical speculations and for still some others, intense poetry. It is no wonder then that the Upaniṣadic philosophy has drawn extreme types of reactions from those who are uninitiated in the Indian cultural tradition. On the one hand there are thinkers like Schopenhauer in whose esteem every line "displays its firm, definite and thoroughgoing harmonious meaning" and from every sentence "deep, original and sublime thoughts arise". On the other hand there are people like W.T. Stace, who, while defending the purity and originality of the occidental thought, goes to the extent of doubting "whether India ever had any philosophy".[3] Here by 'Philosophy in India' most likely he means the Upaniṣadic and Advaitic tradition. He makes this damaging remark on superficial view of the matter and goes on to justify his stand on equally superficial grounds. In his opinion, "The Upaniṣads contain religio-philosophical thinking of a kind, but they should not be called philosophical as they represent man's desire for knowledge as a means towards salvation."[4] In his estimation philosophy stands for pursuing

---

2. *Taittirīya Upaniṣad* II. 9.1.
3. W.T. Stace, *A Critical History of Greek Philosophy*, Macmillan and Company, 1920, p.14
4. *Ibid.*

knowledge for its own sake. As "the roots of Indian thought lie in anxiety of the individual to escape from the calamities of existence", it at best can be called a religion. Besides, philosophy must be rooted in 'wonder' not in soteriology. Then he proceeds on to claim that such type of thinking is definitely not a rational enterprise. It is nothing but "passing out of the realm of thought, reason and philosophy into the dream-and-shadow land of . . . mysticism, where the heavy scent of beautiful poison flower drug the intellect and obliterate thought in a blissful languorous repose".[5]

Stace's second justification for doubting the philosophical status of Indian thought is still more 'violent'. According to him Upaniṣadic philosophy never "rises from the sensuous to pure thought". The basis of his opinion is the use of metaphors, analogies and allegories. Never mind Stace's use of metaphors like 'poison-flower' and 'drugging' of the intellect. This sort of assessment of a tradition amounts to 'intellectual violence'. In order to even criticise an opposing philosophical position one needs to understand it clearly and dispassionately. However, Stace is not the only philosopher to look down upon Indian tradition. There are many. But I chose to refer to W.T. Stace because his remarks appear in the book where he is dealing with Greek philosophy and especially Plato who is well-known for his use of metaphors and myths.

In recent times we also come across a similar misunderstood version of Indian mysticism in the writing of R.C. Zachner, the former Spalding Professor of Eastern Religions and Ethics, Oxford University. Some of his concerns are original yet some appear to be very superfluous. According to him the so-called perennial philosophy of union of opposites as in the Upaniṣads, "needs to be rigorously checked by the rational mind, which it would destroy".[6] Somehow a deep impression is anchored in the

---

5. *Ibid*, p. 371
6. *Our Savage God*, Collins, London, 1974, p. 102

Western psyche that Indian philosophical thought has nothing to do with reason, logic and hence 'thought'.

Such remarks have provoked some eminent contemporary Indian philosophers to take up the cudgels to interpret the non-dualistic philosophical tradition of India in a rational and logical manner. The task of demystification was pioneered by some philosophers in the 60's, and G. Misra is one of them. In the esteemed opinion of J.N. Mohanty, "Misra may well have been the first philosopher to use the technique of Analytical Philosophy for interpretation of Indian Philosophy".[7]

The meta-philosophical position of Misra is that the proper method of philosophy should be nothing other than conceptual analysis. Following Śamkara's distinction between the methods of empirical knowledge (*vyāvahārika*) and philosophical knowledge (*Pāramārthika tattva bhedakatā*) and his thesis that the philosophical knowledge is achieved through *sabda-pramāṇa*, Misra construes *śabda-pramāṇa* as the method of conceptual analysis and this alone as the method of philosophy. Thus he opines that by this method of *śabda-pramaṇa* Śaṁkara lays bare the structure of meaningful discourse, the ground of intelligibility of our conceptual framework. So Misra very boldly claims that Advaita does not indulge in the psychological analysis nor in the mystical experience of *Brahman*. Philosophical knowledge is a knowledge acquired through the examination of the depth-grammar of the discourse. Many of us may disagree with Misra's thesis. But he makes a sincere effort to show that the Advaitic tradition is not non-rational and non-logical in its approach. Prior to Misra's application of the logico-linguistic method, some modern Indian thinkers have tried to interpret the Upaniṣadic concepts like *avidyā* and *adhyasa* in modern psychological perspective. But Misra feels that such attempts do sheer injustice to the philosophical acumen of the ancient Indian

7. *Language, Reality and Analysis* ed. J.N. Mohanty, E.H. Brill, Leiden, 1990, p.1

thinkers.

We notice that in the 50's and the 60's, some Indian philosophers have shown great eagerness to prove the philosophical power of Indian tradition by presenting it in Western philosophical perspective. Whether their method was right or wrong is to be judged by posterity. But one thing is clear that they wanted to prove to the Western world that the Indian tradition is not a form of 'woolly' dogmatism. But all these interpreters believed in discounting mysticism as a part of Indian tradition.

In the subsequent decades we notice a new confidence in Indian thinkers who face the charge of mysticism with a certain amount of nonchalance. They do not feel apologetic about the use of the word 'mysticism' in the context of ancient Indian tradition. Rather they admit that Indian philosophy, especially the brand of philosophy propagated by the Upaniṣads, Śaṁkara and Nāgārjuna, are indeed mystical; but theirs is a mysticism of a different kind. There is nothing irrational or dogmatic about Indian mysticism. Here I take up for discussion two representative thinkers — B.K. Matilal and R.K. Puligandla. The former is moderate in his approach, whereas the latter is vociferous.

B.K. Matilal in his inaugural lecture, delivered in the University of Oxford as the Spalding Professor of Eastern Religions and Ethics, entitled '*The Logical Illumination of Mysticism*', presents Indian mysticism in a rational perspective. He mostly refers to the misgivings expressed by his predecessor R.C. Zachner about the non-rational and non-ethical nature of Indian mysticism. He observes: "The idea of mysticism has mystified many of us including Professor Zachner".[8] He clarifies that 'mysticism', often taken in the negative if not in a derogatory sense in the West, is "overwhelmingly God-oriented", or else is regarded as dealing

8. *The Logical Illumination of Indian Mysticism*, Oxford University Press, Delhi, p.5

with the occult. But the metaphysical foundation of the Eastern mysticism is centred upon the beliefs expressed as 'All is One and One is All' and 'The One is, All else illusion' (*Ibid.* p. 4) And ultimately this One transcends categorial and conceptual understanding. If this is the mark of mysticism, Advaita as well as Mādhyamika philosophy, often charged with mysticism, are based on rigorous rational analysis and dialectics. Both Nāgārjuna and the Advaitic thinkers like Śaṁkara and Śriharsa were astute logicians, in the sense that they used "formal arguments — Indian Syllogistic forms, to be sure — at almost every step of their discourse. They clothed their doctrines in a technical (logical) vocabulary that presupposed a thoroughgoing and systematic training in logic and *pramāṇa-śastra*".[9] Besides, these philosophers were "in fact writing for the intelligent and critical minded readers, and not pleading for the silence of mystic communion." Matilal illustrates his points by referring to two standard texts of the Mādhyamika and Advaita Schools, viz. Śriharsa's *Khaṇḍana Khaṇḍa* and Nāgārjuna's *Vigraha Vyāvartanī*. While referring to the Upaniṣadic literature he admits that some passages of these treatises being enigmatic, there is "naturally a danger that uncritical appraisal of these texts may degenerate into inanities". But "the critical philosophers of India, who were mystically inclined, often made mysticism philosophically attractive and intellectually stimulating".[10] The mystical philosophers of India all along made it clear that there are two different levels of reality, the provisional or conventional (*vyāvahārika* and *pāramārthika*, for Advaitins, *samvṛtti* and *prajñā* for Mādhyamikas, and *aparā* and *parā* for the Upaniṣads). The conventional and provisional level is expressible as they come within the fold of the conceptual and categorial structure. But the 'real' is elusive and ineffable. To the question — why do then these philosophers use logic and language analysis, Matilal's

9. *Ibid.*, p.6
10. *Ibid.*, p. 23

answer is, "the logical arguments are useful, for they illuminate the mystical instead of deepening its mystery . . . one needs the fish trap if one hopes to catch the fish at all. You can kick the ladder away only when you have climbed up the wall or, to use the analogy mentioned by Chandrakīrti, one can forget the raft after one has crossed to the shore".[11] If this leads to mysticism then it is inescapable, but Matilal prefers to call it "cognitive mysticism",[12] a brand totally different from the western conception of it as something irrational, muddle-headed, superstitious, illogical and even non-moral.

Regarding Zachner's charge of amorality, Matilal contends that the soretorial nature of non-dualism and mysticism does not imply moral ambivalence. This type of philosophy never suggests that men should abandon the good-evil distinction to achieve liberation. Rather, in the Indian tradition the question of value is never treated separately from the question of salvation. "The mystic simply claims that when one realises the ultimate reality —the 'cosmic consciousness'—the good-evil distinction sloughs itself off as an inessential and unnecessary detail, for 'evil has been overcome' and without 'evil' 'good' loses its original meaning."

Matilal, by his own admission, is a critic of monism and his philosophical conviction is different. But R.K. Puligandla is a committed Advaitin. Therefore, there is some amount of non-chalance in his defense of Indian mysticism. He in this series of lectures delivered at Utkal University defends mysticism to the hilt. He declares, "it is mysticism, at once pure and simple, most exalted and simply unsurpassed and unsurpassable". But what sort of mysticism is he defending? For 'mysticism' has been interpreted in different ways even by different Indian thinkers. For Puligandla, the mystic is a man "who transcends all categorial framework in the quest of the ultimate reality". Taken in this

---

11. *Ibid.*, p.24
12. *Logic, Language and Reality*, Motilal Banarsidas, Delhi, 1985, p.317

sense the Upaniṣadic seers as well as Śaṁkara and Nāgārjuna are mystics. If this is the criterion of mystical thought then neither the Upaniṣads nor these two schools of philosophy have anything to do with 'irrationality and titillation with the occult'. The most important feature of Indian mysticism is that it has nothing to do with a belief in a creator, preserver and destroyer. It is not theistic — in any sense of the term. No doubt, the mystical literature may rely heavily on the use of acute metaphors, analogies and phenomenological observations. This is usually the characteristic of the mythic discourses involving Gods, etc. But the basic purpose of Indian mysticism is not to arouse dogmatic faith in God, but "to awaken and inspire the listener to orient his mind towards the quest of the *Brahman*". But Puligandla, unlike other defenders of Indian philosophy, does not shy away from admitting that "in our tradition, in particular Upaniṣadic, there is no sharp line of demarcation between philosophy and religion". Yet by religion he does not mean God centric theology. Religion rather stands for spiritualism and a man's quest for the realisation of the highest vision. Puligandla very emphatically clarifies, "contrary to the widespread but mistaken view that in order to live a profound religious life one has to believe in God, the *Upaniṣads* teach with transparent clarity and unrelenting rationality that profound religious life can only arise out of transcending dualism, including that of theism versus atheism and of immanence verses transcendence".

As far as the *jñāna mārga* is concerned Puligandla clarifies that the Upaniṣads (e.g. *Muṇḍaka Upaniṣad*) have always made a clear distinction between the lower and higher levels of knowledge. The perceptual conceptual truths, which even includes the knowledge of the scriptures, are called *aparāvidyā*. These type of knowledge yields truths generated from some categorial framework or other. In contrast higher truth is unconditioned, non-perceptual, non-conceptual and hence non-categorial. But does this not sound like Bradley's Absolutism? Puligandla will say a clear 'No' to this. For him be it Bradley or be it Derrida, nowhere the path of knowledge (*jñānamārga*) is explored in terms of total withdrawal from the level of language. Derrida, the exponent of the now famous theory of deconstruction, like Saṁkara points out that in the whole philosophical tradition there is a heavy reliance on logocentrism. Philosophers, Derrida points out, have been stuck at the level of the binaries, i.e., pair of opposites such as identity and difference, self and the other, being and becoming. The error that they have committed amounts to the elevation of a particular member of the pair to the privileged and exalted status of the Reality. Derrida's suggested path of escaping the trap is 'by staying within the language, but on the middle path between the opposites'. But Śaṁkara's *jñāna-mārga* is a total transcendence of the binaries created by the conceptual and categorial nature of language. This is achieved through the method *of adhyāropa-apavāda.* This "means advancing an argument and then rescinding it at the end; one advances an argument, in order to inspire and orient the listener, and one finally rescinds the argument signalling that neither the premises nor the conclusions of the arguments are to be understood literally". The knowledge of the ultimate truth is achieved through non-conceptual use of language. In this context one finds nothing puzzling about the use of contradictory descriptions of *Brahman* in the Upaniṣads such as "It moves, It moves not. It is the nearest, It is the farthest" etc. Nāgārjuna also aims at such non-conceptual understanding through his critic of the *catuṣkoṭi.* From such an analysis Puligandla proves that Saṁkara and Nāgārjuna are "both profound philosophers and religious seekers in the sense of a mystic".

Many modern critics of Indian philosophy may not agree with Puligandla's version of Advaita and Upaniṣadic philosophy and his defense of mysticism; but have philosophers ever agreed?

Utkal University **Tandra Patnaik**
20 April 1997

1

Immanence and Transcendence in the Upaniṣadic Teaching

THE chief objective of this chapter is to show that the thesis that ultimate reality is at once immanent and transcendent is the central theme of the Upaniṣadic teaching. To the best of my knowledge and belief, in no other tradition does this theme receive such prominence and emphasis as in the Upaniṣadic tradition. I wish to make it clear at the very outset that my defense of the above thesis is not based upon any of the three well-known schools of *Vedānta* philosophy—interpretations of the Upaniṣads. It is my considered judgement that the Upanisadic teaching is thoroughgoingly non-dualistic, and for this reason I do regard Śaṅkara's *Advaita-Vedānta* as the most faithful explication of the Upaniṣads. This does not, however, mean that I shall appeal to Śaṅkara's works in support of my own defense of the thesis that the heartbeat of the teaching of the Upaniṣads is that ultimate reality is at once immanent and transcendent.

What exactly is the Upaniṣadic teaching? The Upaniṣadic teaching can be expressed through two concepts and a proposition. *Brahman* is the power whose varieties of manifestation are the worlds of phenomena, within as well as without the human being. Let me immediately clarify what I mean by 'phenomenon'. A 'phenomenon' is anything that is or can, in principle, be an object of consciousness. It follows from this that every phenomenon can be assigned either both spatial and temporal co-ordinates or just a temporal co-ordinate. Thus, all so-called external phenomena, such as tables, chairs, insects, stars, galaxies, etc., are both in space and time; and, on the other hand, all so-called internal phenomena, such as thoughts, emotions, feelings, mental images, etc., are only in time. It is clear, then, that all phenomena exist in time, although some phenomena also exist in space. In short, all existents are timebound. This is another way of saying that all phenomena arise and pass away; and *Brahman*, the Upaniṣads teach, is the power whose myriad manifestations are the phenomena, external as well as internal. *Brahman* is unborn, uncreated, undying, and hence eternal and immortal. Further, *Brahman* is neither a creator nor a he nor a she, but the *that* (*tat*). *Brahman* cannot be perceived by the senses and the mind; this is to say that *Brahman* transcends the senses and the intellect. *Brahman* is thus imperceivable, inconceivable, and inexpressible. Put differently, *Brahman* is not one among many phenomena and is hence formless and nameless (to be a phenomenon is to have a form and consequently a name).

Atman, like *Brahman*, is unborn, uncreated, undying, and hence eternal and immortal. *Ātman* is pure, objectless consciousness. It is worth emphasizing here that *ātman* is not to be identified with either the empirical ego (*jīva*) or the so-called soul. The reason for this is that the *jīva* is through and through phenomenal and is therefore a timebound existent, subject to arising and passing away. To say that the *jīva* is phenomenal is to say that the *jīva* is an *object* of consciousness, not consciousness itself. *Ātman* cannot be identified with soul either, because the term 'soul', as understood in the traditions in which it is central and prominent, means an individual, immortal entity and yet created; and the term 'soul' is used in the plural — that is, there exist many souls — whereas, in sharp contrast, *ātman* is single, unitary, and, more correctly, non-dual. In short, there cannot be many *ātmans*. Thus, *Ātman* is not to be mistaken for a soul. I, therefore, suggest that, as far as the Upaniṣadic teaching is concerned, it is best to altogether dispense with the term 'soul'

If one were to present the concept of soul to an Upaniṣadic sage, the sage would reject it as absurd, by exclaiming, 'how can something created be immortal?' The point of all these observations is that it is a grave error to identify *ātman* either with the *jīva* or with the soul.[1] *Ātman*, like *Brahman*, is formless and hence nameless, and therefore not one alongside many phenomena. That is, *ātman* transcends space, time, the senses and the intellect, and is therefore, like *Brahman*, imperceivable, inconceivable and inexpressible.

Does this mean, then, that, according to the Upaniṣads, there are two ultimate realities, namely, *Brahman* and *ātman*? Certainly not, for the Upaniṣads reject the notion of two ultimates as uncritical, absurd, and indefensible (remember the trials and tribulations of Sāṁkhya). The Upaniṣads resoundingly teach and unwaveringly maintain that ultimate reality is through and through non-dual. It is important to note that the non-dualism of the Upaniṣads is not to be mistaken for monism, of one kind or another. *Ātman* and *Brahman* are not two numerically distinguishable realities; rather, they are non-different, one and

1. It should be emphasized that from an ontological standpoint, since there can be nothing other than *Brahman* (*ātman*), the *jīva* is non-different from *ātman*; that is, the *jīva* can have no existence apart from *ātman*. This point is further clarified through an analogy. Thus imagine an actor, John, who plays different roles in different plays; one day he plays the role of Alexander the Great, another day that of Julius Caesar, and so on. The spectators of the plays, no matter how many times they see John's performances, will not and cannot know John the actor himself, apart from his roles: The roles are the appearances of John but not John himself. Nevertheless, these appearances, no matter how many, do not have independent status apart from John; that is, the Alexander and the Caesar one sees on the stage have no existence of their own — they have no being independently of the being of John. In a similar manner, the *jīva* is an appearance of *ātman*, having no existence of its own, independently of the existence of *ātman*; and just as it is a mark of ignorance to identify John with a role in which he appears, say Alexander, so also it is a mark of ignorance to identify *ātman* with the *jīva*.

the same (like the morning star and the evening star), and this is the central proposition of the Upaniṣadic teaching. Another way of saying this is that the terms '*Ātman*' and '*Brahman*' are two different labels for one and the same non-dual reality. When we are awake, dreaming, or sound asleep, whatever is experienced (that is, is an object of consciousness) is but a manifestation of the power that is *Brahman*; and when one brings mental modifications to a cessation, there no longer are any objects of consciousness, but just consciousness itself; this pure, objectless consciousness is indeed the *ātman*, which is none other than the unmanifest *Brahman*. In terms of contingency and necessity, *ātman* is the necessary being, the being that no one has the power to get rid of, and all phenomena — objects of consciousness — are contingent, in the sense that they need not have existed. *Ātman* is not contingent, in the sense that *ātman* cannot conceivably not exist, cannot be eliminated, cannot be gotten rid of. How so? Because *atman*, consciousness, is required for getting rid of anything. When the manifestations of *Brahman* disappear, *Brahman* does not disappear but becomes unmanifest and the unmanifest *Brahman* is none other than *ātman*, the sole, non-dual reality. Thus the terms '*Ātman*' and '*Brahman*' are but two different labels for one and the same non-dual reality.

From what has been said thus far, it should abundantly be clear that the central teaching of the Upaniṣads is that *Brahman* is the ultimate non-dual reality, and since *Brahman* and *ātman* are non-different the ultimate non-dual reality is also pure, objectless consciousness. *Brahman* is immanent, in the sense that all existents, actual as well as possible, are but the variety and multiplicity of the manifestations of *Brahman*. *Brahman* is transcendent, in the sense that *Brahman*, either as the power whose manifestations are the worlds of phenomena or as pure, objectless consciousness, cannot, in principle, be experienced as a phenomenon, an object of consciousness. Let me state clearly, right here and now, that the term 'transcendent' in the Upanisadic context does not mean something outside of the world (whatever that means), beyond the ken and pale of the human being: on the contrary, it means that which cannot be experienced as a phenomenon. *Brahman* is fully experienceable, in two senses: all objects — phenomena —, actual and possible, are but the manifestations of *Brahman*, and *Brahman* as unmanifest is pure, objectless consciousness. And it is unquestionably true that we experience various phenomena, and the Upaniṣads exhort us to realize that these phenomena are none other than the power that is *Brahman*; and *Brahman* as unmanifest, pure, objectless consciousness is experienceable when one eliminates all mental modifications, that is, when one stills the mind. The former is the experience of *Brahman* as immanent and the latter of *Brahman* as transcendent. It should be emphasized that in the experience of *Brahman* as transcendent there can be no distinctions among the knower, the known, and the act of knowing. That is, these distinctions belong in the domain of dualistic ways of knowing, but not in the experience of *Brahman*, the non-dual reality. In the experience of *Brahman* as transcendent, there is nothing but objectless consciousness, and there is knowledge of neither the knower nor the known nor the act of knowing. Someone might now feel provoked to remark, in a tone of objection, 'This sounds like mysticism'. Let me respond by saying, 'Yes, it is not something that sounds like mysticism, but rather *is* mysticism, at once pure and simple, most exalted, and simply unsurpassed and unsurpassable.' However the term 'mysticism' may be understood in other traditions, one thing is clear: in the Upaniṣadic teaching, mysticism has nothing to do with irrationality and titillation with the occult; Upaniṣadic mysticism is concerned with the authentic, existential realization of ultimate reality as the non-dual *Brahman*, *ātman*. Let it also be noted that the Upaniṣadic teaching and mysticism have nothing to do with belief in a creator-preserver-destroyer god or gods. The sole and exclusive concern of the Upaniṣads is knowledge of the ultimate non-dual reality.

I come now to the *mahāvākyas* (great pronouncements and

declarations), which are the foundation for the analysis and defense of the central Upaniṣadic teaching. The point here is that if one comprehends that the *mahāvākyas* are the profound phenomenological-analytical truths, then one comprehends the truth of the Upaniṣadic teaching that the ultimate non-dual reality, *Brahman* (*ātman*), is at once immanent and transcendent. Here are the *mahāvākyas*, scattered throughout the Upaniṣads and so well-known that I shall not clutter this paper with superfluous footnotes:[2] (1) *tad ekam* (That One), (2) *sarvam khalvidam brahman* (All this is *Brahman*), (3) *advitīyam* (That without a second), (4) *prajñānam brahma* (*Brahman* is pure, objectless consciousness), (5) *ayam ātma brahma* (This Self is *Brahman*), and (6) *aham brahmāsmi* (I am *Brahman*). The first three of these are the assertion that whatever is or can be, the actual and the possible, is *Brahman*; nothing can exist besides *Brahman*, everything is *Brahman*, there can be nothing other than *Brahman*. It is clear from this assertion that *Brahman* is the totality of existence, actual and potential. Now someone might object to this way of understanding the term '*Brahman*'. My reply is to ask that someone as to what alternative (and purportedly more adequate) definition of '*Brahman*' can he propose. I am saying in no uncertain terms that there can, in principle, be no alternative definition which can withstand scrutiny and analysis. Thus consider someone proposing to define '*Brahman*' as the totality of physical (material) existence; but what is one to do with other modes of existence, say, the mental and the emotional? The only recourse one has is either to deny there exist the mental and the emotional or to acknowledge their existence and argue that the mental and the emotional are eventually—ultimately—reducible to the physical, the material. The first alternative is not worthy of any serious consideration; as for the second, although it is laudable for its desire and consequent quest for a single reality to which all phenomena can

2. *The Upaniṣadas*, tr. by Swami Nikhilananda; four volumes, Advaita Ashrama, Calcutta, India.

ultimately be reduced, it is unfortunately seriously flawed. What the advocate of reductionism, whether physicalistic (materialistic) or mentalistic (idealistic), fails to inquire into is the following question: if the physical, mental, and the emotional are all *equally phenomena* (objects of consciousness), what grounds are there for one to think that one of them is primary and fundamental and the others secondary and derivative? The proponent of reductionism has absolutely no rational grounds for thinking so. His advocacy of reductionism, of one kind or another, is purely due to his attitude, preference, biases or plain ignorance. This kind of reductionism cannot, in principle, succeed, because if all kinds of phenomena are reducible to some one kind of phenomena, whatever it may be, I can always rationally ask as to what this kind of phenomena are reducible to. Let me emphasize that this question is perfectly sensible and significant; for, after all, what are phenomena? Phenomena, as has been pointed out earlier, are timebound existents, that is, they are ineluctably subject to arising and passing away; this in turn means that phenomena are composite and hence non-self-existents. And, this is the point here, with regard to any and all phenomena one can always intelligibly ask as to what they are constituted of. Thus the view that all phenomena are reducible to some one kind of phenomena is uncritical and misguided. In keen contrast, with great insight and wisdom, the Upaniṣads teach, 'Yes, all phenomena, without exception, are reducible to *Brahman*, which, bear in mind, is *not* Itself a phenomenon.' This is to say that *Brahman*, as the power whose countless manifestations are phenomena, is transcendent; try to imagine, visualize, and picture this *Brahman*, and you will see that your mind returns wholly baffled; on the other hand, if *Brahman* were a phenomenon, of whatever kind, one would have succeeded in imagining, visualizing, and picturing *Brahman*. Transcendent *Brahman* is the unmanifest power, and being unmanifest, It bears no marks, and therefore transcends (cannot be captured by) the senses and the intellect. Thus, That to which all phenomena are ultimately reducible cannot Itself be a phenomenon, and to think otherwise is the height of ignorance (*avidyā*) and unwisdom. The purpose of all these observations, then, is to drive home the point that simple-minded reductionism, of whatever kind, is doomed to failure; the reason for this is that it is rooted in the profound error of thinking that whatever it is to which all kinds of phenomena are reducible is itself a phenomenon, that is, in a flawed conception of ultimate reality.[3] It should also be clear from this brief discussion that the term '*Brahman*' cannot be defined and understood in any way other than as the totality of existence, actual and possible, and this is precisely the import, the essence, and the heart of the *mahāvākya* that *Brahman* is that without a second.

I shall now briefly deal with the *mahāvākya*, 'All this is Brahman'. Let me immediately point out that there can be no clearer statement of the immanence of ultimate reality, *Brahman*, than this one. Thus consider any two phenomena, say *A* and *B*. According to the declaration that all this is *Brahman*, it follows that each of these phenomena is *Brahman*. Now one might raise the objection: 'If, as the Upaniṣads teach, phenomenon *A* is identical with *Brahman* and phenomenon B is identical with *Brahman*, then it logically follows that *A* is identical with *B*. But, as a matter of fact, *A* (a tree) is not identical with *B* (a bird). Hence the contradiction, and the thesis that all this is *Brahman* is simply false.' This objection is based on a serious misunderstanding of the Upaniṣadic teaching; in particular, it confounds immanence and transcendence of *Brahman*. Yes, phenomena *A* and *B* are not identical; they are certainly not identical *as phenomena*, manifestations of *Brahman* (*Brahman* as immanent); but they are each perfectly and fully identical with *Brahman*, the power whose manifestations they are; the power that manifests Itself as

3. Ramakrishna Puligandla, "Is the Central Upanishadic Teaching a Reductionist Thesis?", *Asian Philosophy*, Nottingham, U.K., 1991, Vol. 1, No. 1, pp. 15-20.

A is one and the same power that is manifested as *B*. If this were not so, *Brahman* would not be That without a second, *advitīyam*; and since there cannot, in principle, be any thing other than *Brahman*, whatever is or can be is *Brahman*, *Brahman* as transcendent. In other words, plurality and non-identity hold with regard to *Brahman* as immanent, and identity and non-duality hold with regard to *Brahman* as transcendent. Only by failing to grasp this point, can one raise the above objection.

Before proceeding to discuss the proposition that *Brahman* and *ātman* are non-different, I wish to make a few salient remarks. I am often amazed to hear people describe the Upaniṣadic teaching as 'substance-ontology'. Many think that the Upaniṣads teach that *Brahman*, ultimate reality, is a substance, 'substance' being understood in the Western, Aristotelian sense of that which remains unchanged in time. I submit that this is a grave error. To the best of my knowledge and belief, nowhere in the Upaniṣads is *Brahman* described as 'substance'. If anything, we are untiringly told that *Brahman* is formless, nameless, imperceivable, inconceivable, inexpressible, and devoid of any and all attributes and relations. In the light of this, how can anyone claim that the Upaniṣads uphold a substance-ontology? 'Substance' is a category — a name, essentially — and if *Brahman* is nameless, as the Upaniṣads maintain, how can one describe *Brahman* as substance? Categories, for example, substance, process, attribute, relation, cause, effect, etc., apply only to manifest *Brahman*, to phenomena, but not to *Brahman* as transcendent. And there is no need to emphasize that it is *Brahman* as transcendent that the Upaniṣads speak of as nameless, formless, imperceivable, inconceivable, and inexpressible. Moreover, if anything is a substance, it must possess (or be capable of possessing) attributes, and we are told again and again that *Brahman* is wholly devoid of properties. Thus, to think of *Brahman* as substance is a serious error. Further, when we examine the definition of 'substance', we notice that it refers to time and timebound existence; for what does it mean to say that 'substance' is that which remains *unchanged in time*? The irony of this definition is that, according to it, substance both exists in time and remains unchanged in time. But everything that exists in time is necessarily subject to change. In a word, the whole conception of substance is absurd and senseless. I am not hereby denying that the various categories, including that of substance, are useful; rather, I am only pointing out that these categories are perfectly useful when we study various segments of the world of phenomena from different categorial frameworks and do not apply to *Brahman* as transcendent, the ultimate non-dual reality. This is the point of the Upaniṣadic pronouncement that *Brahman* transcends the senses and the intellect, imperceivable, inconceivable, and inexpressible. Is this not also the heart of the *Nāsadīyasūkta*, the so-called hymn of negation?

I am fully aware that there are passages in the Upaniṣads which speak of *Brahman* as unchanging and eternal. How is one to understand these passages? Let me immediately emphasize that the point of using the term 'unchanging' is not to proclaim that *Brahman* is a substance, but rather to contrast *Brahman* as transcendent with *Brahman* as immanent, varieties of phenomena. It is the hallmark of every phenomenon to be subject to change; and when some passages talk about *Brahman* as unchanging, it is to call attention to the truth that the category 'change' which applies to all phenomena does not apply to *Brahman* as transcendent, the ultimate non-dual reality. Thus the statement that *Brahman* is unchanging is to be correctly understood as tantamount to the statement that *Brahman* is not one among many phenomena, not that *Brahman* is a substance. It is pertinent to examine here what the pronouncement that *Brahman* is eternal means. To say that *Brahman* is eternal is not to say that *Brahman* is of an enormously long duration, but rather to say that *Brahman* is *timeless*, and this is precisely what is meant by saying that *Brahman* is unborn, uncreated, and undying. Birth, creation, and death characterize phenomena, timebound existence, and *Brahman* is simply uncharacterizable because *Brahman* as transcendent is not timebound, not a phenomenon, but eternal. And if *Brahman* is eternal, in the sense of being timeless, it is surely absurd to describe *Brahman* by any term, including 'substance', 'change', and 'lack of change'. Thus *Brahman* is *not* a substance; in fact, Brahman is not any *thing* or *entity* at all. In a word, Brahman is *no-thingness*.

On what grounds do the Upaniṣads proclaim that *Brahman* and *ātman* are non-different, one and the same? Let me first dispel some serious misunderstandings concerning consciousness. In the Western tradition, the terms 'consciousness', 'mind', 'I', and 'self' are used synonymously. Thus remember Descartes saying, 'What then am I? A thinking thing. And if I entirely cease to think, I altogether cease to exist.'[4] The point to be made here is that in the Upaniṣadic teaching mind and consciousness are not the same; mind is through and through phenomenal, that is, it is an object of consciousness; and, like all other phenomena, it is subject to change (a timebound existent). And it is quite amusing to hear people talk about levels of consciousness, expanding consciousness, raising consciousness, and so on. There are even books with the title 'Structure of Consciousness', whose authors undoubtedly consider themselves to be those fortunate few, who have attained the most profound insights into consciousness and are eager and ready to teach and enlighten the ignorant and the unfortunate. According to the Upaniṣadic teaching, which I uphold (on phenomenological-experimental-analytical grounds), this kind of talk is unmistakable testimony to massive and pervasive *avidyā* (ignorance). Consciousness, not being a phenomenon (I have heard professors of philosophy, psychology, and religion use such phrases as 'the *phenomenon* of consciousness'), does not and cannot have any *structure*. Consciousness is formless and hence nameless. One cannot

4. Rene Descartes, *Meditation II*.

expand, compress, raise, and lower consciousness. The phrase expanding consciousness' can only mean enlarging the *range* of objects of consciousness. One cannot do anything to consciousness, because it is not an entity, a timebound existent. Consciousness, like *Brahman*, is *no-thingness*.

Let us begin with the question: When one thinks away everything that can be thought away,what is left, what is the ultimate residuum? Once again, I should point out a fundamental difference between the Upaniṣadic teaching and the Western tradition. Many Western thinkers believe and teach that mind cannot be stilled. I submit that this belief is not based upon any phenomenological-experimental -analytical investigation; rather, it is *merely* a belief, uncritical and unexamined. For, is it not true that Kant teaches that the noumenal is for ever inaccessible to the human being? Has he not taught that the human being has only sensible but not intellectual intuition? I ask, on behalf of the Upaniṣadic seers, how does Kant know this? How has he come to know that mind cannot be stilled? These are questions that can be answered not with clever definitions but only on the basis of systematic phenomenological investigation. And I am firmly maintaining that *Yoga* is indeed such an investigation. And what is *Yoga*? *Yoga*, as Patanjali tells us in his great work, *The Yoga-Sūtras*, is *citta-vṛtti-nirodha*, cessation of mental modifications. And when everything that can be thought away is thought away, what remains is pure, objectless consciousness, the ultimate residuum. This is precisely what I mean by saying that consciousness is the necessary being, whereas objects of consciousness, actual and potential, are contingent beings, that is, they can be thought away. Thus when mind is stilled, all phenomena disappear; that is, there are no *manifestations* of *Brahman*. *Brahman* now is unmanifest; and to say that *Brahman* is unmanifest is not to say that *Brahman* vanishes away, becomes non-being. How so? Because *Brahman*, not being a phenomenon, a timebound existent, neither comes into being nor vanishes away. With the cessation of mental modifications, one does not experience manifest *Brahman*. The unmanifest *Brahman* is none other than the ultimate residuum, *ātman*, pure, objectless consciousness. And when all objects have vanished away and if *Brahman* does not become non-being, then whatever is left as the ultimate residuum is indeed *Brahman*. Let me emphasize here that everything that can properly be said of *Brahman*, of course only negatively, can also properly be said of *ātman*. Thus both *ātman* and *Brahman* are formless and nameless, transcend the senses and the intellect, and are nothingness. They are non-dual in two senses: nothing can exist other than *Brahman* (*ātman*), and neither *Brahman* nor *ātman* is composite, that is, constituted of parts. In a word, *Brahman* (*ātman*) is impartite. It is in the light of these phenomenological considerations that the *Upaniṣads* teach that *ātman* and *Brahman* are non-different, one and the same.

Before bringing this chapter to a close, I wish to make a few pertinent observations. That ultimate reality is at once immanent and transcendent can be rationally maintained only in a thoroughgoingly non-dualistic teaching, which is the crowning glory of the Upaniṣadic tradition. Such a teaching cannot consistently be maintained in *any* dualistic tradition, for example, the theistic religious traditions of the West and dualistic philosophies such as that of Descartes. Thus consider Judaism, Christianity, and Islam. According to these religions, God is at once the creator of the world and *wholly* transcends the world, His creation. Therefore, God, for ever, is beyond the ken and pale of the human being, for ever inaccessible to the human being; but what is interesting here is that the adherents of these religions also claim that in the beginning only God was, and nothing else; and then God made the world *ex nihilo*, from nothing. From the Upanisadic standpoint, such a view presents God as a cheap stage-magician who pulls a rabbit, a parrot, and sometimes even a college professor out of an allegedly empty hat. If, as per their claim, in the beginning (whatever that means) only God was and nothing else, is it not rational to think that God made the world out of Himself (Herself!) — God became the world? The point here is that to say that God made the world out of nothing is absurd and irrational. But if God *became* the world, then one should be able to say, 'all this is God'. But the followers of these religions rail against any such statement by exclaiming, with a sense of shock and horror, 'Oh, that's pantheism', as if there were something terribly wrong with and sacrilegious about pantheism. If the world were created by a God who *wholly* transcends his creation, the Upaniṣadic seers want to know why we should have anhything to do with such a God. And I cannot conceal my sense of amazement at the fact that many people, including scholars, regard Rudolf Otto's *Idea of the Holy* as a great work. In contrast, I consider it a second-rate work at best, because, according to Otto, God is *the wholly other*, *ganz ander*. And he thinks that this is the most sublime truth. I shall not go here into any detailed critique of Otto's claims, but only point out that Otto never bothered to inquire as to how any relation can obtain between two *wholly, radically* different entities, namely, God and the human being. But he is quite comfortable with proclaiming that God is at once the creator of the world — and creation is a relation — and is nevertheless the *ganz ander*, the wholly other. The Upaniṣads surely reject such a claim as absurd and irrational. One should now be able to clearly see why simultaneous immanence and transcendence is a serious problem to any dualistic tradition, whether of the West or of the East. In stark contrast, in the Upaniṣadic teaching, *Brahman* is *not* God; nor is *Brahman* a He or a She. *Brahman* is existence, actual and potential. Nothing can exist apart from, other than, *Brahman*; hence the declaration, 'all this is *Brahman*'. As such, holiness and sacredness are not the exclusive attributes of some mysterious God, wholly other than the world, but rather the entire universe is suffused with holiness and sacredness. Thus, when the Upaniṣadic *ṛṣi* sees a bird fly over, he sees it as a manifestation of *Brahman*, as a bearer and revealer of the power and mystery that is *Brahman*. Many Westerners, including scholars, describe the Upanisadic teaching as 'pantheism', and we have already alluded to their sense of horror at pantheism. Let me make it perfectly clear that it is palpably wrong and positively misleading to describe the Upanishadic teaching as 'pantheism', for *Brahman* is *not* God, as understood in dualistic, theistic traditions, Western or Indian. Would it be correct, then, to call the Upaniṣadic teaching 'panBrahmanism'? No, because it is redundant; and why is it redundant? Because, if, as the Upanisads teach, *Brahman* is everything, nothing can exist other than *Brahman*, what is the point of the prefix 'pan'? None whatever. Hence the Upanisadic teaching is most faithfully and appropriately called 'Brahmanism', pure and simple. And *Brahman* is not something wholly transcendent to the world; on the contrary, *Brahman* is fully immanent, transparent, and clearly visible, audible, and so on. Further, *Brahman* is pure, objectless consciousness, which at once is the transcendent and unmanifest *Brahman*.

Why is mysticism at the very heart of the Upaniṣadic teaching but frowned upon in the dualistic, theistic traditions of the West? The answer is clear and straightforward: Upaniṣadic mysticism is but the direct consequence of the teaching that *Brahman* (*ātman*), the ultimate non-dual reality, is at once immanent and transcendent. Is it any wonder, then, that in the Upaniṣadic tradition it is the pinnacle of achievement, the highest wisdom, for one to arrive at the point where one can rejoicingly proclaim, 'I am *Brahman*', and in the West such a proclamation is nothing short of blasphemy? Is it any wonder, then, that in the dualistic, theistic traditions of the West mysticism was vehemently discouraged, held in the utmost contempt, denigrated, decried, and belittled, and mystics such as Meister Eckhart and Al Halaj were systematically persecuted, excommunicated, and even tortured and put to death? These are but the bitter fruits of the absurd thesis of ultimate dualism. Let it be noted that even today the terms 'mystic', 'mysticism', and 'mystical' are used in the West to dismiss someone or something as irrational, muddleheaded, superstitious, anti-social, and immoral.

One of the most profound insights of the Upaniṣadic teaching concerns the principle of two kinds of knowledge and truth. This principle was formulated in the *Muṇḍaka Upaniṣad* and may be expressed as follows: There are two kinds of knowledge and truth, the lower and the higher, *aparā* and *parā vidyā*. All perceptual-conceptual truths are lower, relative, conditioned, mundane truths, *vyāvahārika-satya*; these truths are the product of our perceptual-conceptual activities; that is, they are inextricably bound up with our psycho-physiological constitution, and it is natural that beings constituted differently will advance different claims as to what the world is like. The truths proclaimed by all rational inquiries, including the sciences, are lower truths, and it is a serious mistake to lay absolute claims on them. To put it differently, all lower truths are categorial truths, that is, truths generated from some categorial framework or other.[5] It is truly remarkable that the *Muṇḍaka Upaniṣad* declares that even the Vedas are lower truths.[6] And I know of no other tradition which proclaims even its own scriptures to be lower truths. In contrast, the higher truth (*pāramārthika-satya*) is absolute, unconditioned, supramundane, and non-perceptual and non-conceptual, and therefore cannot be captured in any categorial framework. It is to be realized in direct, non-dual intuition (*prajñā*). Notice that there are many lower truths, whereas there can only be one higher truth. What is the reason for this? There are many phenomena and many different categorial frameworks and hence

5. For a detailed discussion of categorial frameworks and the nature of categorial knowledge and truth, see Ramakrishna Puligandla, *Jñāna-Yoga (The Way of Knowledge): An Analytical Interpretation*, New Delhi, D.K. Printworld Pvt. Ltd., Indian edition, 1997.

6. *Mundaka Upaniṣad*, I. i. 4-6.

many lower truths. And since *Brahman* as transcendent is the non-dual reality, besides which nothing can be, there can only be one higher truth. It is worth noting that whereas truth and being are separable in the case of every lower truth, no such separation is possible with the higher truth; that is, here Truth and Being are non-different, one and the same. Thus when one brings mental modifications to a cessation, there are no objects of consciousness, but only objectless consciousness; this objectless consciousness, *ātman*, is at once Truth and Being, and this is precisely what is meant by saying that knowledge of *Brahman* transcends the tripartite distinction of the knower-known-act of knowing, a distinction characteristic of all lower (dualistic) knowing (and knowledge). Moreover, lower knowledge and truth lack the power to radically transform the human being — as witness people quite accomplished in some branch or other of lower knowledge suffering from anger, jealousy, depression, angst, fear of death and capable of cruelty and violence toward others and even themselves. In contrast, the higher knowledge and truth are soteriological, in that they have the power to radically transform the human being from one of ignorance and disease to one of knowledge, peace, fearlessness, freedom, and wisdom. Why is it that there has never been in the Upaniṣadic tradition the conflict, strife, and warfare between science and religious quest? My answer: the principle of two kinds of knowledge and truth. Wherever this principle is absent, for example, the dualistic, theistic traditions of the West, conflict between science and religion is inevitable. Such conflict is essentially due to mistaking of some lower truth or other for the higher truth. Thus, the Darwinian theory of evolution, which was and in some quarters till is, the center of stormy controversy in the West, produced no commotion or agitation at all in India. As one traditional *pandit* told the great biologist Sir J.B.S. Haldane, 'Darwin, in proclaiming the theory of evolution, had gone quite far but not far enough; for, after all, he only proclaimed the essential unity of all life-forms, whereas our Upaniṣadic forefathers had long ago taught the essential unity of all existence.' Such, then, is the power of the Upaṇiṣadic teaching that *Brahman*, the ultimate non-dual reality, is at once immanent and transcendent.

To conclude: (1) the central Upaniṣadic teaching is the thesis that the ultimate non-dual reality, *Brahman* (*ātman*), is at once immanent and transcendent; (2) the variety and multiplicity of the world of phenomena are but the myriad manifestations of the imperceivable, inconceivable, and inexpressible power that is *Brahman*; (3) as the various phenomena, actual and possible, *Brahman* is immanent; (4) as the power whose manifestations are the worlds of phenomena, *Brahman* is transcendent; (5) *Brahman* as transcendent is indeed the *atman*, pure, objectless consciousness; (6) followers of the Upaniṣadic teaching, in particular the principle of two kinds of knowledge and truth, have nothing to fear from science and other rational inquiries; on the contrary, like art, science and other rational inquiries are to be celebrated as resounding testimony to the creativity of the human spirit; the domain of all rational inquiries, including the sciences, is the phenomenal, the categorial, the perceptual-conceptual — in a word, the dualistic. Mistaking lower truths for the higher truth has grave and disastrous consequences — as witness the history of dualistic, theistic religions, full of animosity, hostility, and bloodshed; (7) yes, the Upaniṣadic teaching is thoroughgoing reductionism, as different from simple-minded, ignorant, and dogmatic reductionism, such as the physicalistic and the mentalistic; (8) the Upaniṣadic teaching is mysticism, *par excellence*, not only unsurpassed but unsurpassable; the Upanishadic mysticism has nothing whatever to do with denigration of rationality and glorification of irrationality; nor has it anything to do with preoccupation with superstitions and the occult; (9) one hears these days of deconstructing metaphysics, overcoming metaphysics, and so on; a study of the Upanisads clearly shows that true, full, and complete deconstruction of metaphysics can only be achieved through non-duality, but not through any form of dualism; and (10) contrary to the widespread but mistaken view that in order to live a genuinely profound religious life one has to believe in a God, the Upaniṣads teach with transparent clarity and unrelenting rationality that profound religious life can only arise out of transcending all dualisms, including that of theism-versus-atheism and of immanence-versus-transcendence. For, after all, if one has known *Brahman*, what use has one for theism and atheism? None whatsoever.

2

Science, Philosophy and Religion
Quest for a Unitary Vision

LET me begin by calling attention to the fact that in the non-Western traditions in general and in the Indian tradition in particular science, philosophy, and religion were never sharply demarcated; and it is quite instructive to note that a similar situation prevailed in the Western civilization for a long time. But with the advent of modern philosophy and science, science, philosophy, and religion began to be sharply demarcated in the West; and under the influence of Western civilization these lines of demarcation also became entrenched in the minds of Western-educated non-Westerners, Indians included; and since the potential readership of this lecture consists of Indians and Westerners, I thought it appropriate here to deal with the vexatious question whether science, philosophy, and religion are totally disparate or any relationship obtains among them. I propose to show that the widespread view that science, philosophy, and religion are clearly demarcatable and hence are in principle opposed, incompatible, and irreconcilable is based on ignorance (*avidyā*) and the attendant ailments of blindness, intolerance, and dogmatism. I shall further show that there is a vision, a unitary vision, in which science, philosophy, and religion, as facets and dimensions of human experience, are harmoniously accommodated and integrated, thereby leading to a life of knowledge — *jñāna* — wisdom, freedom, peace, and joy, individually and collectively.

In order to clarify the concept of knowledge, whether in science, philosophy, or religion, I shall introduce the notion of categorial framework. All thinking begins somewhere and where it begins depends upon the background of the thinker and the sorts of things the thinker is interested in inquiring into. Thus it is only natural that some things are included while others are excluded from one's inquiry. By the term 'categorial framework', I mean the matrix in which inquiry takes place and knowledge-claims are advanced. A categorial framework thus underlies every system of knowledge, whether in science, philosophy, or religion. Every categorial framework consists of certain pre-suppositions, concepts, categories, definitions, axioms, postulates, a system of logic, and criteria for judging the truth or falsity of knowledge-claims and hence for their acceptance or rejection. Further, every categorial framework is associated with (or points to) a certain world-view. Thus, for example, one can speak of the Platonic, Aristotelian, Augustinian, Sāṁkhyan, Nyāya-Vaiśeṣika, Jaina, Buddhist, Vedāntic, Hegelian, Bergsonian, Whiteheadian categorial frameworks. It is worth noting here that it is usually philosophers who construct, articulate, and defend particular categorial frameworks. A philosopher who constructs a categorial framework also attempts to justify it. Such a justification, following Kant, is known as 'transcendental deduction'. Transcendental deduction consists of showing that (1) the particular categorial framework under consideration is the one actually employed by people to gather objective knowledge of the world, and (2) the categorial framework is the only one capable of enabling us to obtain objective knowledge of the world (uniqueness-demonstration).

Before proceeding further, it will be in order to distinguish three levels of knowledge. Level-1 consists of knowledge of objects (phenomena) constituting a certain domain, for example, physics, and the various specialities within physics, such as astronomy, low-temperature physics, nuclear physics, and so on; or biology and the many specialities therein. Level -2 consists of knowledge of the foundations of a given discipline at Level-1, foundations in the sense that they make possible the discipline (give rise to and support the discipline) and lend to the discipline its specific form, content, and character. In the light of our earlier characterization of a categorial framework, the foundations of any discipline at Level-1 may be referred to as 'categorical framework'. Someone may be a physicist in the sense of one who investigates some subset(s) of phenomena constituting the domain of physics; but he or she may not have inquired into the foundations of his or her own discipline and therefore may either be wholly unaware of its foundations or only have vague and unclear notions about them. Most scientists, including some very successful ones, are of this kind. This remark is not to be construed as an insult or accusation but only as a statement of fact. However, it is often the case that only those scientists who also inquire into the foundations of their disciplines make original and radical contributions to the advancement of their fields — for example, Galileo, Newton, Darwin, Einstein, Bohr, Schrodinger, Heisenberg, to mention only a few of the truly great scientists. Level-3 goes beyond knowledge of particular categorial frameworks underlying particular disciplines to knowledge of the nature of categorial frameworks in general and thereby of the nature of knowledge producible by categorial frameworks. Knowledge based on categorial frameworks may simply be called 'categorial knowledge'. Level-3 knowledge, then, is knowledge concerning the nature of all categorial knowledge — of categorial knowledge in general.

I shall also refer to a categorial framework as a 'perceptual-conceptual framework'. The notion of categorial framework stems from the insight that the kind of knowledge a certain kind of beings are capable of producing is inextricably bound up with their psycho-physiological makeup. This means, first, that among various kinds of beings human beings constitute only one;

and second, the nature and limits of *human* knowledge is governed by the physiological and psychological constitution of the human being. This is the same as saying that had human beings been of a different psycho-physiological makeup than their present one, the nature and limits of knowledge they produce would be different (from that which they now, as a matter of fact, produce). There should be nothing surprising about this claim; for simply imagine our optic nerves being arranged differently; then it is only to be expected that our experience of colours would have been different from our present experience of them. Similar is the case with regard to our other sense-organs. It is obvious, then, that our perceptions are ineluctably bound up with the constitution of our perceptual apparatus. To take another example, we are the kind of beings who cannot see the back of an object simultaneously with its front.That is, if I hold up an object,say a book, in front of you, you can only see its front and not its back. There is nothing mysterious about this observation; on the contrary, it is a correct report about our ways of perceiving. We also know that changes in our bio-chemical makeup result in changes in our perceptions. It is a fact, then, that our perceptions are a function of our physiological constitution. Our claims as to what sorts of things make up the world and what properties they possess, and what relations obtain among them is a function of our physiological makeup.

But, in addition to our physiological makeup, our psychological constitution determines the nature of the knowledge we produce. The term 'psychological' here is to be understood as encompassing the mental and the emotional. In short, the psychological consists of the sentient and sapient, the emotional and the mental, respectively. What comes to us through our sense-organs is ordered and organized — categorized — according to our psychological constitution. It goes without saying that beings endowed with a different psychological constitution than we are will organize and categorize differently what they receive through their sense-organs, thereby resulting in knowledge-claims different from ours. It is to be noted that our psychological makeup allows for a variety of ways of organizing and categorizing, each way being appropriate to a certain end and purpose. All the possible different ways of ordering, organizing, and categorizing that which comes through our sensory channels and equipment define the 'range of our psychological makeup'.

It should be clear from the above that as human beings we are capable of perceptions and conceptions, actual and potential, lying within a certain range determined by our psycho-physiological constitution. We may refer to this range as 'perceptual-conceptual range'.

The knowledge-claims a thinker advances are constituted of percepts and concepts allowed for (permitted by, falling within the range of) the categorial framework with which he conducts his inquiry. This is the reason a categorial framework may be referred to as 'perceptual-conceptual framework'.

In light of the above, we are now in a position to make the following fundamental observations concerning the nature of categorial knowledge.

1. All rational-scientific knowledge is through and through categorial knowledge; by this I mean that every expressible and communicable knowledge-claim, whether in science, philosophy, or religion, is necessarily (inevitably) bound up with some categorial framework or other. This is the same as saying that no expressible and communicable knowledge-claim is in principle possible apart from and independently of some categorial framework; that is, every expressible and communicable knowledge-claim is relative to a categorial framework.

2. It would therefore be a serious mistake to lay absolute claims on behalf of any categorial knowledge.

3. However, each thinker, being ignorant of this fact, makes absolute claims on behalf of knowledge generated by his own categorial framework and condemns the knowledge-claims of other thinkers (conducting their inquiries with different frameworks) as false.

4. In this manner arise conflict and opposition among thinkers; thus simply imagine the battles being constantly waged against each other by thinkers, Western or Indian — Aristotelians against Platonists, Humeans against Kantians, Idealists against realists, substance-philosophers against process-philosophers, empiricists against rationalists, theists against atheists, Western philosophers against non-Western philosophers, and so on. It is to be emphasized that, contrary to the widespread but uncritical belief, such conflicts also exist in the scientific enterprise — as witness the opposition between Ptolemic astronomy (geocentric system) and Copernican astronomy (heliocentric system), between Aristotelian physics and the physics of Galileo and Newton, between Newtonian physics and Einsteinian physics, between classical physics and quantum physics, between Creationism and Darwinian biology, and so on. The conflict between one system (theory) and another is ultimately traceable to the conflict and incompatibility between the world-views — paradigms — underlying the systems. The term 'paradigm' is generally used when one talks about conflicts between competing scientific theories. A paradigm is essentially a categorial framework, although it is worth emphasizing that, rigorously speaking, a categorial framework is much wider than a paradigm, in the sense that a categorial framework encompasses a paradigm (and not the converse).

5. Transcendental deductions of categorial frameworks are in principle impossible. Although it is quite easy, through sociological research, to show that, as a matter of fact,

people use a certain framework to produce objective knowledge of the world, the second part of transcendental deduction — uniqueness-demonstration — cannot be accomplished. Uniqueness-demonstration consists of showing that a certain categorial framework is the *only* framework which enables us to produce objective knowledge of the world. The advocate of the framework cannot, in principle, establish this, and every argument to establish this is necessarily (inevitably) circular and therefore question-begging and fruitless. For, in order to demonstrate that the world is as described by his own framework, the thinker needs to know what the world is like independently of his framework, and then show that his framework does indeed describe the world faithfully. Is it not true that if I showed you a photograph and asked whether it is a picture of my friend John Bubblehead, you cannot answer unless you have seen him at least once? Just so, unless one knows what the world is like independently of categorial frameworks, one cannot sensibly claim that the world is indeed as described by one's own framework. And for this reason, every argument the thinker constructs for demonstrating the uniqueness-claim necessarily employs the categories of the very framework (for, on his own admission, there is none else), which in the first place needs justification. The incontrovertible conclusion, then, is that transcendental deductions are in principle impossible and also circular.

6. It should be quite clear by now that, broadly speaking, scientific knowledge is Level-1 knowledge. Philosophical inquiry is concerned with the construction and examination of particular categorical frameworks; and the knowledge-claims of philosophers are also categorial; however, there is a fundamental difference between the knowledge-claims of science and those of philosophy: a philosopher, unlike a scientist, is usually concerned with saying something

about ultimate reality, and he does this by elevating some category of his framework to an ultimate status. Hence such philosophical proclamations as: ultimate reality is of the nature of substance, of the nature of process, ultimate reality is of the essence of mind, of spirit, ultimate reality is material (constituted of elementary particles), ultimate reality is one, ultimate reality is plural, ultimate reality is a person, and so on. But the point here is that philosophical inquiry is essentially inquiry at Level-2 knowledge. We shall examine later the nature and significance of knowledge at Level-3.

7. To say that all scientific-rational truths are bound up with some framework or other is to say that they are all relative truths; 'relative' here is to be understood as relative to a framework and hence to beings of a certain psycho-physiological constitution. But there are many who uncritically equate relative truth with falsehood. 'Relative truth' means truth certifiable by all inquirers who are similarly constituted and conduct their inquiry according to a certain categorial framework. Thus, for example, when an American physicist advances a knowledge-claim, say, electrons are negatively charged particles, a Japanese physicist, operating with the same framework with which the American physicist operates, certifies that knowledge-claim to be true. It is to be emphasized that a knowledge-claim has neither meaning nor truth (nor falsity) apart from a categorial framework. Thus objective truth is not truth which has nothing to do with us but rather is truth certifiable by different inquirers who are constituted alike and conduct their inquiry according to a certain framework. Put pointedly, objective truth is no more and no less than intersubjective truth.

8. What about universal truth? Once again, many people mistakenly equate universal truth with absolute truth.

> Universal truth is relative truth that has received over a period of time certification by larger and larger number of inquirers the world over. 'Universal truth' is not absolute truth, for 'absolute truth' means truth that is independent of the constitutions of the inquirers and hence independent of any and all categorial frameworks. In light of our characterization of categorial framework, it follows that there simply cannot be any categorial truth which can be claimed to be absolute truth. If there is any absolute truth at all, one thing must be very clear: it cannot be captured in any categorial framework by any inquirer. That is, absolute truth, if there be such, transcends all categorial frameworks of all inquirers, here as well as elsewhere. Only those who are ignorant of the nature of categorial knowledge mistake some categorial truth for absolute truth.

I come now to a discussion of knowledge at Level-3. We have earlier stated that knowledge at Level-3 consists of knowledge of the nature of categorial knowledge in general — knowledge producible through any and all categorial frameworks. Thus all the points listed above are part and parcel of knowledge at Level-3. Philosophers do not usually conduct inquriy into Level-3 knowledge, for they are too absorbed in and preoccupied with defending their own frameworks and laying absolute claims on behalf of their own categorial knowledge-calims, thereby becoming embroiled in interminable philosophical controversies, disputes, and disagreements. But in the Indian tradition, there are two most illustrious thinkers known for their profound insight into and analysis of the nature of all categorial frameworks and hence of all categorial knowledge. I am referring to Nāgārjuna and Śaṅkara, of the Mādhyamaka and Advaita-Vedānta respectively. One of the central insights and teachings of these sages is that we superimpose names and forms (*nāma* and *rūpa*, concepts and percepts) on a formless and nameless reality and thereby generate categorial frameworks and categorial truths. The activity of superimposition is known in Śaṅkara as *adhyāsa*. It is obvious that *adhyāsa* is the source of all categorial frameworks, and the superimpositional activities of differently constituted beings result in different categorial frameworks and therewith different knowledge-claims. Further, both Nāgārjuna and Śaṅkara teach that there are two kinds of knowledge and truth, *saṁvṛtti-satya* (*vyāvahārika-satya*) and *pāramārthika-satya*. *Saṁvṛtti-satya* is lower, relative, conditioned, mundane truth, and *pāramārthika-satya* is the higher, unconditioned, absolute, supramundane truth. Through relentless analyses of categories and categorial frameworks, Nāgārjuna *shows* that all categorial truths are lower truths; and if someone makes an absolute claim on behalf of any categorial truth, we can show, by using the categories, principles, and rules accepted by the advocate himself, that such a claim leads to contradiction and absurdity; and since the advocate of the claim accepts freedom from contradiction as a necessary condition for a claim to be accepted as truth, the thinker has now to withdraw his claim. But what drives a thinker in the first place to make absolute claims on behalf of a catagorial truth? According to Nāgārjuna, it is ignorance of the nature of categorial truths and attachment to one's own categorial framework that drive the thinker to lay absolute claims on behalf of a categorial truth. One feels secure and assured in so far as one's framework is secure and assured; and any attack on one's framework is deemed as an attack on oneself. In this manner ignorance gives rise to blindness, intolerance, and dogmatism, which, in turn, produce pain and suffering (*duḥkha*). Thus it is attachment, born out of ignorance, to one's own framework that brings one pain and suffering. Only by commanding insight into the nature of categorial frameworks and categorial truths does one free oneself from attachment and therewith from pain and suffering.

It is worth noting here that there are many lower truths, whereas there is only one higher truth. Every lower truth is a categorial — perceptual-conceptual — truth. It is certifiable through perceptual-conceptual inquiries, methods, and procedures. Further, in the case of every lower truth, truth and being are separable. Thus consider, for example, the claim that a certain planet has two satellites. This claim will be regarded as true provided there exists a certain state of affairs (being); the truth of the claim and the state of affairs that makes the claim true are clearly separable. However, in the case of the higher truth no such separation is possible; the reason for this is that, unlike lower truths, the higher truth cannot be captured through percepts and concepts — categorial framework; quite to the contrary, the higher truth can only be experienced in direct, immediate, non-perceptual and non-conceptual intuition (*prajñā*); the reason for this is that, in the case of the higher truth, truth and being are non-different, one and the same. It is not as though there is truth on the one hand and its certification through a state of affairs on the other. Here truth and being are one and the same. Put another way, the higher truth cannot be apprehended as an *object* of consciousness; in coming to know the higher truth, the distinctions characteristic of every lower truth, namely, the knower, known, and the act of knowing, simply vanish away. This is precisely what is meant by saying that in regard to *pāramārthika-satya*, one's being is the truth, one's being is the reality, *ātman* is *Brahman*. Thus, in the experience of the higher truth, there can be neither propositions nor state of affairs bestowing truth upon propositions. In a word, the higher truth transcends the senses and the mind — percepts and concepts, forms and names. The point of all these observations is that insight into the nature of categorial knowledge points to the higher truth — ultimate, transcendent reality — the direct experience of which is sought by the religious. One would naturally like to ask whether Nāgārjuna and Śaṅkara are philosophers or religious seekers. The answer is that each of them is both a profound philosopher and a religious seeker, in the sense of a mystic ('mystic' here is to be understood in the sense of one who transcends all categorial frameworks in quest of ultimate reality).

When we survey the history of religions, we notice that it is full of dogmatism, intolerance, fanaticism, bloodshed, and unspeakable horrors and cruelty. This is more so in the history of Western religions than that of non-Western religions, the Indian ones in particular. What is the reason for this sad and tragic state of affairs? In the light of our discussion of categorial frameworks and categorial knowledge, the answer should be clear and straightforward. Each people lays absolute claims on behalf of its own religion and condemns those of others as false and dangerous, deserving only to be eliminated. In this manner arise religious wars and forced conversions. What went wrong? One fails to realize that one's own religion is the result of a certain superimpositional activity, a categorial framework, determined by a variety of factors such as language, geography, socio-political circumstances, and so on; and one makes absolute and exclusive claims for the truth of one's own religion. Hence arise conflict and opposition, resulting in wars and the attendant pain and suffering. In other words, religious conflict is a direct consequence of ignorance (*avidyā*) of the nature of categorial knowledge. Thus knowledge of the nature of categorial knowledge in general liberates one from the shackles of attachment, dogmatism, fanaticism, and intolerance and makes possible the pursuit and attainment of the higher truth — knowledge of the ultimate reality and one's true being, resulting in wisdom, freedom, peace, and joy.

What has all this to do with science? Is it possible to formulate a vision in which science, philosophy, and religion are harmoniously accommodated and integrated? Let us begin by noting that science itself points to a transcendent reality. Science cannot, in principle, explain the world as a whole. By this I mean that science cannot give us any coherent account of how the world came to be. For, in order to explain how the world came to be, one needs to know the conditions and circumstances (if one is permitted to talk in this way at all) *prior* to the world's coming to be; and there seems to be no way in which one can gain knowledge of these conditions and circumstances. But the fact that there is a world at all forces us to acknowledge a transcendent reality — reality that transcends capture by science (categorial frameworks). Let me illustrate this point in some detail. Consider the so-called Big Bang theory. According to this theory, there originally was a singularity — a primordial black hole — with whose explosion came into being space, time, and matter. It is worth noting here that the Big Bang theory is very similar to the Sāṁkhya account of the evolution of unmanifest *prakṛti* into the world of space, time, and matter. But the question is: what caused the Big Bang? There is no answer to this question, for, as we earlier pointed out, in order to answer this question one needs to know the conditions and circumstances prior to the Big Bang. But science itself tells us that all our concepts and principles of space, time, and matter break down within (!) the singularity and therefore we cannot know what caused the Big Bang; scientists can only offer interesting conjectures and suggestions; and the most interesting conjecture is that the Big Bang was caused by spontaneous quantum fluctuations. Does this really answer the question? Some scientists offer cosmologies of ever-expanding universe, others of an oscillating universe (Big Crunch followed by a Big Bang), and so on. It is worth emphasizing here that the Sāṁkhyan also finds himself in the same predicament, of not being able to explain as to what triggered the evolution of the unmanifest *prakṛti* in a state of perfect dynamic equilibrium. And we all know that some Sāṁkhyans appealed to a God (Supreme *puruṣa*), while others were content to confess their ignorance. Science investigates various segments of the world of our senses and mind — phenomena — by constructing categorial frameworks. But the world as a whole is not an object of our experience, actual or possible, and therefore any question about the world as a whole transcends all categorial frameworks, including those of scientific investigation. In any case, the important point here is that there is a reality which defies investigation through rational-scientific procedures. Thus all cosmologies, including modern ones, are essentially stories (and this is inevitably so) and are not to be taken literally. I am not hereby suggesting that scientists stop constructing stories — cosmological theories — for the stories, although they never enable us to answer the question we discussed above, are in themselves interesting and occasionally serve as heuristic devices in shedding light upon aspects of inquiry, leading to fruitful answers to questions other than that of the origins of the world. It is to be noted that even if science were able to offer a satisfactory (scientifically) explanation of the origins of the world, there would still be the question as to why there is anything at all rather than nothing. For, after all, there has to be something in the first place for us to ask for an explanation. In short, the existence of the world is a mystery. This is what Śaṅkara means when he says that in the last analysis the existence of the world is inexplicable (*anirvacanīya*). If *Brahman* is the sole reality and nothing other than *Brahman* exists, how is it possible to explain the existence of *Brahman*? And since, according to the Upaniṣads, *Brahman* is non-different from the world, our inability to explain why there is *Brahman* is at once our inability to explain the existence of the world. Argument, explanation, and proof belong in the domain of duality and plurality (premises and conclusion, explanation and the explained, proof and the proven). But if *Brahman* is the totality of existence, actual and potential, reality beside which nothing exists, no explanation, scientific, philosophic, or religious, of the existence of *Brahman* (the world as a whole) is in principle possible. Put differently, there cannot, in principle, be an all-encompassing categorial framework. A categorial framework, by its very nature, is sustained by the tension between what it includes and what it excludes. Where there is no such tension, there cannot be any categorial framework; thus an all-encompassing framework simply collapses under its own weight and will be wholly non-functional and useless.

Conflict and opposition between science and religion are traceable to ignorance (*avidyā*), first, as to the nature of categorial knowledge, and, second, as to the differences in the goals and purposes of categorial frameworks in scientific and religious inquiries. It would be a grave error to think of science and religion as rivals and competitors; science is concerned with the investigation of the world of our senses and the mind, whereas religion is the quest for the transcendent, which eludes capture by any framework. Scientific treatises and religious scriptures do not belong in the same shelf, for they have different agenda. Science is concerned with producing knowledge of the world of phenomena, whereas religion is concerned with the salvation (*mokṣa, nirvāṇa*) of the human being. Science should not think of itself as being concerned with bringing salvation, and religion should not think of itself as being concerned with producing and enhancing scientific knowledge. Has anyone heard Jesus teaching people the correct astronomical, geological, and biological theories? If knowing the correct scientific theories is essential to the salvation of human beings, would such a compassionate being not have taught us? Jesus is concerned with offering salvatory knowledge, not scientific theories. This brings me to the discussion of how religious scriptures are to be read.

One must first understand that scriptures, insofar as they are couched in language, are based on categorial frameworks. But since the true concern of religious inquiry is the quest for the transcendent and since the transcendent cannot be captured in any framework, one should not attempt to understand scriptures in a literal fashion. Taking them literally only results in conflict with science; further, there are the most dangerous consequences of literal-mindedness in matters religious. such as blindness, fanaticism, dogmatism, intolerance, and so on, which will only serve to lead the person astray from the true religious quest and become embroiled in battles with science and religions other than one's own — as witness the self-proclaimed religious people still busy dragging Darwin to courts. These people think they are being religious and serving God by opposing scientific theories they regard as a threat and challenge to their scriptures (of course according to their own misguided understanding of scriptures as well as science). Where is the quest for the transcendent and therewith salvation in all of this? At this point, it is significant to note that the *Muṇḍaka Upaniṣad* regards even the Vedas as lower knowledge, insofar as they are products of language and categorial frameworks, and hence in the last analysis to be trascended. How, then, is a scripture to be read? In order to answer this question, we need first to distinguish two kinds of use of language: conceptual and non-conceptual. Language is used conceptually in all rational-scientific frameworks and discourses. Concepts here have clearly designated referents. That is why, for example, 'electron' is understood by all physicists in the same manner, as referring to a certain entity, an object, a phenomenon. In keen contrast, language is used non-conceptually in scriptures and religious discourse. This is the reason we find in all scriptures rich use of metaphors, analogies, parables, myths, aphorisms, epigrams, didactics, and so on. Thus, for example, neither '*Brahman*' nor '*ātman*' nor 'the Kingdom of God' has any referent. No one can point to something and say, 'that is *Brahman*, that is *ātman*, that is the Kingdom of God (as different from the kingdom of the Devil).' The point here, then, is that scriptures are to be read non-conceptually. That is, the purpose of scriptures is not to provide the reader (the listener) with a huge catalog of facts; in brief, lanugage is not used in a scripture informatively (informative use of language belongs in science) but evocatively. The purpose of scriptures and discourses of religious teachers — sages, seers, and *ṛṣis* — is not to supply the listener with factual -scientific information, but rather to inspire the listener, to awaken the listener to the transcendent reality, and to catapult him, as it were, into a mode of being, radically different from the ordinary, dualistic mode of being. In order to accomplish this, a great teacher employs language with extraordinary skill (*upāya*). It is instructive to call attention here to the distinction between a *paṇḍit* (scholar) and a *guru*: the *paṇḍit* teaches the student the language of scriptures, say

Sanskrit, and supervises his reading of the various texts, and familiarizes him with the associated literature; and when the student performs well in his tests and examinations, the *paṇḍit* gives him the grade and sends him off. The scholarship, and not the salvation (enlightenment), of the student is the primary goal and concern of the *paṇḍit*. In keen contrast, the salvation and enlightenment of the student is the sole and primary concern of the *guru*, textual knowledge being purely secondary, unimportant, and inconsequential. The *guru* is an adept at skilful, non-conceptual use of language; and, besides the skilful, non-conceptual use of language, the *guru* will employ any technique, any procedure — any means — to awaken the student to the transcendent reality; and we all know that Zen masters, with their pedagogy of koans — puzzles, paradoxes, conundrums, mind-freezers — are among *gurus*, *par excellence*. Are Nāgārjuna and Śaṅkara both *puṇḍits* and *gurus*? The answer is a resounding 'Yes'. As *paṇḍits* — scholars and men of learning — through profound and systematic analyses they discovered the nature of categorial knowledge, successfully undertook the quest for direct experience and knowledge of trenscendent reality (*Brahman*, *ātman*, *śūnyatā*), and as *gurus* they inspired and awakened many to the realization of the transcendent reality. It is of the utmost importance to note here that *adhyāropa-apavāda* is the famous pedagogical technique and *modus operandi* of Śaṅkara. This technique consists of offering, in the context of discussions of reality, the best possible rational arguments and eventually withdrawing them. What is the point of withdrawing an argument after it has been so carefully formulated? The argument is withdrawn lest the listener take it literally, for if the listener takes it literally bad things will happen to him. Thus the technique of *adhyāropa-apavāda* goes hand-in-hand with non-conceptual use of language.

Science is perceptual-conceptual knowledge. It is knowledge of the world of our senses and intellect. Scientific knowledge-claims are always tentative, subject to revision, modification, and sometimes even outright rejection. There is no room in the scientific enterprise for finality and absolute truths. Nor is there an absolute categorial framework underlying scientific investigation; for we know that in the history of science there were revolutions resulting in the overthrow and replacement of one framework by another. Through its intrinsic inability to explain the world as a whole — how the world came to be — science points to a transcendent reality which for ever and in principle eludes capture by any framework.

Philosophy is concerned not only with the construction and examination of particular categorial frameworks but also with the investigation of the nature of categorial knowledge in general. Great philosophers, such as Nāgārjuna and Śaṅkara, have shown us that (1) there is indeed a formless, nameless, non-dual reality, on which we superimpose names and forms, thereby generating categorial frameworks; (2) all categorial knowledge, including scientific knowledge, is relative and conditioned; (3) laying absolute claims on behalf of any categorial knowledge-claim unavoidably results in contradiction and absurdity; (4) there cannot, in principle, be an all-encompassing framework; and (5) the transcendent reality cannot be captured in any framework; it can only be experienced in direct, immediate, non-dual intuition (*prajñā*).

The sole goal of religion is to attain direct experience and knowledge of the transcendent reality. Religion is not to see science and philosophy as rivals and competitors. Seeing them as rivals and competitors is a mark of incurable ignorance (*avidyā*), with tragic consequences.

What, then, is the unitary vision that harmonisouly accommodates science, philosophy, and religion? Let us note first that science does not need the support of religion, and *vice-versa*. Scientific knowledge-claims are to be accepted or rejected according to the criteria that are part and parcel of the framework itself, and not by appeal to scriptures and religious pronouncements. Decisions between competing scientific theories are to be arrived at through criteria such as simplicity, elegance, and, above all, pragmatic efficacy, and not through religious considerations. Thus, 'harmonious accommodation' does not mean mutual support; rather, it means: (1) absence of conflict, opposition, and discord and (2) concord and smooth fitting. From our discussion of categorial frameworks, it should be clear that such harmonious accommodation becomes possible only when one realizes that the proper goals and functions of science, philosophy, and religion form a continuum. To cite a few examples, the Big Bang theory and Darwinian evolutionary biology are in harmony with the Indian religious tradition in general; but this does not mean that modern cosmology and biology need the support of Indian tradition, and *vice-versa*; the role of consciousness and the inseparability of the observer and the observed in quantum physics is in full harmony with the teachings of the Upaniṣads; non-local causality (that the world is an interconnected world and not made up of isolated substances) is in full accord with the Buddhist teaching of Dependent Origination—*paṭītya-samutpāda*—and the Upaniṣadic teaching of the common-rootedness of all phenomena in *Brahman*, and so on. It is true that this kind of harmony and accord between science and religion is more common in certain traditions rather than others. The more mystical a religious tradition, the greater is the harmony between the tradition and science; and conflict and discord between science and religion is more common, pronounced, and entrenched in religious traditions in which mysticism does not occupy the central place. There can be no dispute about the claim that mysticism is the most distinguishing trait of Indian religions, orthodox or unorthodox. This is precisely the reason that there has hardly ever been in the Indian civilization the kind of conflicts, opposition, and animosity between science and religion that one finds in the Western civilization. But let it be emphasized that mysticism existed and continues to exist in the West, in spite of circumstances antagonistic to the growth and cultivation of the mystical life. Science, philosophy, and religion are all manifestations of the creativity of the human spirit. All these stem from a single source. the human spirit, and this fact in itself is resounding testimony to the possibility of the unitary vision that I speak of.

3

The Central Upaniṣadic Insights
Their Significance to Deconstruction and Theory of Everything

It is common knowledge that there are many different interpretations of the teachings of the Upaniṣads, the three principal ones being the Advaita-Vedānta of Śaṅkara, the Viśiṣṭādvaita-Vedānta of Rāmānuja, and the Dvaita-Vedānta of Madhva. It is not my concern here to discuss any of these schools of Vedānta; rather, I shall offer my own understanding and interpretation of the central Upaniṣadic teachings, draw out their bearing upon the topic of reality and consciousness, and then go on to discuss the significance of these observations to modern science, including theory of everything and deconstructionism. I should, however, make it clear that I find myself most sympathetic to Śaṅkara's non-dualistic interpretation of the Upaniṣads; the reason for this is that it is my considered judgement that Śaṅkara's interpretation is most faithful to the original Upaniṣadic texts themselves. Accordingly, I find myself in agreement and accord with the fundamental insights underlying Śaṅkara's interpretation. This reference to Śaṅkara becomes clear in my discussion of Derrida's brand of deconstruction.

Without burdening the readers with vain and pedantic notes and references, let me straightforwardly state what I construe to be the central, fundamental, and most significant teachings of the Upaniṣads. Non-dualism (non-dual reality), Advaita, pervades the Upaniṣadic corpus; that is, the basic thrust and main drift of the Upaniṣads is the teaching of non-dual reality, *Brahman*. Leaving aside the subtle and significant distinction between non-dualism and monism, philosophers, Western as well as Indian, sometimes equate the Upaniṣadic teaching of non-dualism with the Parmenidean proclamation of monism. I submit that such an equation only serves to obscure and befuddle the uniquely Upaniṣadic and hence the most distinctive insight and teaching that the non-dual reality is at once non-different from *ātman*, the true self, objectless consciousness. This is to say that the non-dual reality and *ātman* are not two numerically distinguishable realities, but rather 'non-dual reality' and '*ātman*' are two different labels for one and the same reality. In this manner, phenomenological inquiry becomes significant. Thus, for example, in the *Māṇḍūkya Upaniṣad*, the state of deep sleep, besides those of waking and dreaming, comes under phenomenological scrutiny. The point here is that if *ātman* and the non-dual reality are non-different, then knowledge of this reality is none other than knowledge of one's true self as *ātman*, objectless consciousness. To the Upaniṣadic people, that we are conscious beings is the most profound and unceasing mystery. This preoccupation with the fact of consciousness naturally involves phenomenological pursuits, including various techniques and disciplines of meditation. I am here indicating in a broad fashion as to how and why the topic of consciousness is so integral to the Upaniṣadic teaching. One may also want to trace the development in the Vedic literature as a whole to the point of arrival at the central teachings I stated above. But that is not essential for my task here. My main concern is to understand why consciousness occupies such an all-important place in the Upaniṣads and the implications and significance of this fact to phenomenology, construction of philosophical theories (systems, *darśanas*), and therewith the place and role of reason and rationality.

The concept known as '*adhyāsa*' ('superimposition') in Śaṅkara's writings as well as the teaching of two kinds of knowledge and truth is fully treaceable to the Upaniṣads. This concept and this teaching are extremely important in our attempts to understand the meaning of 'knowledge of the non-dual reality'. We are told again and again in the Upaniṣads that *Brahman*, the non-dual reality, is utterly devoid of form, name, attributes, relations, etc., and that the senses and the mind cannot grasp *Brahman* — *Brahman* is imperceivable and inconceivable. Reason and learning, no matter how subtle and elaborate, are not adequate to the attainment of the knowledge of *Brahman*. *Brahman* is to be experienced in *prajñā* — non-dual intuition. This knowledge, by its very nature, is always, unexceptionably, first-hand; it cannot be had second-hand. It is absurd to ask for and await someone else's certification in this matter. Each human being has to obtain this knowledge through his or her own experience, and therefore any talk of certification by others only betrays massive *avidyā*. It should thus be clear that the Upanisads unequivocally declare that knowledge of *Brahman*, the non-dual reality (and hence *ātman*, the true self), cannot be had through the senses and the mind, the senses and the intellect (reason), perception and conception; it can only be attained through *prajñā*, non-dual intuition. In other words, knowledge of *Brahman* cannot be had without transcending the senses and the mind. This brings us to two questions: (1) Are the Upaniṣads philosophical works? Or are they merely religious works? and (2) If the senses and the mind (reason, intellect) are ultimately powerless to reveal reality, what is the point of constructing and advancing several elaborate arguments? It is salient to remind ourselves here of the arguments of the last chapter that in the Indian tradition, in particular the Upaniṣadic, there are no sharp lines of demarcation between philosophy and religion. Yes, many subjects and topics we regard as philosophical, for example, reality and self, are certainly raised and discussed in the Upanisads. But it would be a serious mistake to thereby think that the intent of the Upaniṣads is to advance a philosophical theory of reality; quite to the contrary, the main, predominant, aim of the Upanisadic teaching is the attainment of knowledge of

Brahman. Analogies, metaphors, epigrams, aphorisms, acute phenomenological observations, and sometimes arguments and inferences based on such observations are surely to be found in the Upaniṣads, just as one finds in them mythic discourses involving gods, demons, etc. The point I wish to make here is that the purport of philosophical concepts and arguments is not to furnish the listener with a *theory* of reality but rather to awaken and inspire the listener to and to orient his or her mind toward the quest for *Brahman*, the quest for the true self. I shall go so far as to say that for the Upanisadic teachers any theory, philosophical or otherwise, which succeeds in orienting the mind toward the quest for *Brahman* will do. On the other hand, no theory, no matter how logical, clear, and impressive, is commendable if it fails to awaken one to the quest for *Brahman.* In so far as the attainment of the knowledge of *Brahman* is concerned, the criterion by which to accept or reject a theory is whether or not it has the power to successfully orient the mind of the listener to the quest for *Brahman.* If a theory fails to do this, find some other theory — some other mode of discourse — which does it; and, after the theory has done its job, throw away the theory — do not cling to it or be attached to it. One cannot help being reminded here of the Buddha's parable of the raft. Such, then, is the role of reason in the Upaniṣadic tradition. The Upaniṣads are thus first and foremost mystical treatises; philosophical concepts, theories, arguments, etc. are used, not for constructing and offering some true *picture* of reality, but to inspire and awaken one to the quest for *Brahman.* In light of this, we can easily understand the procedure of *adhyaropa-apavada*, so prominent in Śaṅkara's works. '*Adhyaropa-apavada*' means advancing an argument and rescinding it at the end; one advances an argument in order to inspire and orient the listener, and one finally rescinds the argument signalling that neither the premises nor the conclusion of the argument are to be understood *literally*; for if one takes them literally, paradoxes, puzzles, conundrums and stifling of the mind and reason will inevitably result, and one misses the whole point of the argument, namely, to enable one to launch upon the quest for *Brahman*. That is, if anyone takes the arguments literally, bad things will happen to him or her Another way of making this point is to say that language is used in the Upanisads predominantly non-conceptually. Hence the not infrequent resort to analogy, metaphor, poetic utterances, mythic discourse, and so on. The chief purpose of conceptual use of language is to convey information, to report facts to make knowledge-claims in some domain or other of the world of our senses and intellect; in keen contrast, the sole and paramount purpose of non-conceptual use of language, that of the Upaniṣads, is to orient the mind toward the quest for reality; in brief, to quote my learned friend, the late Professor Troy Organ, conceptual use of language is descriptive and informative, while that of the non-conceptual is motivational and evocative. Thus it would be a grave error to think that the Upaniṣadic teachers — *ṛṣis* — are trying to offer some facts and descriptions of the non-dual reality (*Brahman*), to communicate some information about *ātman* (the true self). I might add here that this distinction between the conceptual and non-conceptual uses of language parallels the distinction, alluded to in the last chapter, between a *paṇḍit* and a *guru*. The former is concerned with imparting information, textual or otherwise; whereas the latter's sole concern is with the enlightenment of the disciple, his attainment of the knowledge of *Brahman*, the non-dual reality.

The teaching of two kinds of truth and knowledge directly follows from the declaration that *Brahman* cannot be realized, captured, and grasped by the senses and reason. Thus the *Mundaka Upaniṣad* distinguishes between *aparā-vidyā* and *para-vidyā*, the lower, mundane, relative, conditioned, perceptual-conceptual knowledge and truth — *vyāvahārika-satya* — and the higher, supramundane, unconditioned, absolute, direct, immediate, intuitive, non-perceptual and non-conceptual knowledge and truth — *pāramārthika satya* — respectively. The former is categorial knowledge and truth, inextricably bound up with some categorial framework or other; the rational as well as the irrational is the domain of this kind of truth and knowledge; in sharp contrast, the latter is transcategorial, transcending the senses and the intellect, and hence inexpressible. It is non-rational. It is worth noting in this context that the *Mundaka Upaniṣad* goes so far as to unwaveringly declare that even the Vedas, including the *mahāvākyas*, are lower knowledge and truth. One's quest for the knowledge of *Brahman* requires that one transcend even the *mahāvākyas*. Performance of rituals and ceremonies is of no avail in the quest for *Brahman*. Attainment of the knowledge of *Brahman* is indeed self-realization.

Śaṅkara certainly employs philosophical concepts and arguments in his interpretation of the Upaniṣads. But it would be a serious error to thereby think that Śaṅkara is primarily a philosopher offering a *theory* of reality. Śaṅkara is primarily a mystic, who employs philosophical concepts and arguments only in order to inspire and illuminate the listener. This does not, however, mean that Śaṅkara is not an original philosophical thinker or that his philosophical formulations cannot be critically examined and evaluated; rather, what it means is that when one examines and evaluates Śaṅkara's philosophy — non-dualistic Vedānta — one should bear in mind and not lose sight of the fact that Śaṅkara's overarching goal and aim is mystical-spiritual, namely, the knowledge of *Brahman* and hence self-realization. Failure to keep this in mind will only result in the grossest of misunderstandings, grotesque distortions, and absurd claims and charges. In a word, Śaṅkara is not a mere *pandit* but is essentially and primarily a *guru*, in the true sense of the Upanisadic *ṛṣis*.

Before discussing deconstruction, I wish to make some observations in order to dispel certain chronic, persistent, widespread, and profound misunderstandings as regards the Upanisadic teaching and Śaṅkara's interpretation. Philosophers, Western as well as Indian, describe Śaṅkara's interpretaions of the Upaniṣads as 'substance-philosophy' and 'substance-ontology' Such claims, I humbly submit, are the direct consequence of one's not realizing that Śaṅkara is primarily a spiritual teacher and only secondarily a philosopher. *Brahman* and *ātman*, it has been claimed by commentators on the Upaniṣads and Śaṅkara, are substances. Is this claim justified? I have maintained that there is absolutely no justification for the claim. Nowhere in the Upaniṣads has it been said that *Brahman* (*ātman*) is a substance. If anything, we are untiringly told that *Brahman* is formless and nameless, wholly devoid of attributes and relations. If so, how can anyone say that the Upanisads teach that Brahman (*ātman*) is a substance? 'Substance' is a category — a name, if you will — and as such it cannot be applied to *Brahman*, the non-dual reality. *Brahman* is imperceivable, inconceivable, and inexpressible, transcending the senses and the mind, perception and conception, senses and reason, logic and illogic — the rational and the irrational. Many philosophers say that they base this claim on such Upaniṣadic passages which declare that *Brahman* is unchanging, eternal, and immortal. Yes, there can be no denying that there actually are passages in the Upaniṣads (and Śaṅkara) which read, '*Brahman* is unchanging'. My point is that 'unchanging' here is not meant to convey that *Brahman* is substance, either Aristotelian, Cartesian, or Nyāya-Vaiśeṣikan; rather, the purport of such phrases is to contrast *Brahman* with its appearances — phenomena — whose hallmark is arising and passing away, that is, change. It is the height of *avidyā* to take 'unchanging' in this context to mean that *Brahman* is a substance; for if *Brahman* is a substance, how are we to make sense of the oft-repeated Upaniṣadic declaration that *Brahman* is formless and nameless, imperceivable and inconceivable, and inexpressible? And, let me emphasize, it is this theme that runs throughout the Upaniṣads. This fact alone is sufficient to warn us against such errors as taking 'unchanging' in the sense of substance. Substance possesses attributes, and attributes can only be possessed in timebound existence; so substance, like attributes, is timebound. And if 'substance' is taken as not timebound, then the puzzle and paradox arises as to how something unchanging and not timebound comes to possess attributes, clearly timebound and changing. This consideration alone should alert us against the error of understanding '*Brahman* as unchanging', as a substance. Language is used here non-conceptually, to awaken in us the intuition and understanding that *Brahman* transcends time, *Brahman* is timeless, and 'eternity' means not a long stretch (duration) of time, but rather timelessness. This is precisely the meaning in which *Brahman* is said to be unborn, uncreated, undying, immortal, and eternal. Birth, creation, death (mortality) — beginnings and ends — have their basis in time. Thus the point of the Upaniṣadic declaration that *Brahman* is unchanging is not that *Brahman* is a substance but rather that *Brahman* transcends all concepts, including those of change and permanence — substance and process, being and becoming. This is the only understanding that is in full accord with the central teaching that *Brahman* is imperceivable, inconceivable, and inexpressible. But if one does not realize that the Upaniṣadic seers and Śaṅkara are primarily mystics and that their chief goal is to bring about spiritual transformation in the listeners, then one is bound to make the mistake of interpreting their teachings as if they were mere philosophical propositions expounding an ontology opposed to the ontologies proposed by other philosophers.

Adhyāsa (superimposition) is the activity of superimposing on the formless and nameless non-dual reality (*Brahman*) names and forms — percepts and concepts, *rūpa* and *nāma*. According to the Upaniṣads and Śaṅkara, superimposition is the manifestation of *avidyā* (ignorance concerning reality, the true self). And language is the prime instrument of superimposition. Thus superimposition conceals and distorts reality — *āvaraṇa* and *vikṣepa*. The various theories of reality constructed by philosophers, then, according to the Upaniṣad only serve to detract us from the fundamental spiritual goal of self-realization.

realization of *Brahman*, *ātman*, the non-dual reality. It is only when one fully and thoroughly disengages oneself from superimposition — from language — does one open oneself to the experience of *Brahman*. I shall refer to such disengagement as 'desuperimposition'. Hence *adhyārōpa-apavāda*. It is clear, then, that desuperimposition is nothing short of rejecting all theories of reality as positively misleading and woefully inadequate for the realization of *Brahman*. This is the meaning of 'deconstruction' in the Upaniṣadic context.

Does this mean, then, that the Upanisads and Śaṅkara have altogether failed to recognize the positive and constructive role of language, reason, and rationality? Certainly not; for the principle of two kinds of knowledge and truth is not possible unless one recognizes the lower (categorial) truths, which are the product of language, perception, and conception, reason, and rationality. Lower truths are truths pertaining to the manifestations (appearances) of *Brahman* and they are essential for effectively dealing with phenomena, and these truths are to be judged in the final analysis according to their pragmatic efficacy in ordering, understanding, and manipulating phenomena. Manifestations of *Brahman* are strung upon and held together by language — speech and writing. Thus, while using language, reason, and rationality in dealing with phenomena, one should be free from the delusion that one can also comprehend and experience *Brahman* through language. And since the Upaniṣadic seers are primarily concerned with experience of *Brahman*, it is only natural that they should place such great emphasis upon desuperimposition and eschewing language and theorizing altogether. This attitude toward language is thus not accidental, but essential and integral to a tradition in which mysticism — experience of reality and not talk about reality — is pivotal.

I come now to a comparison of Derrida's deconstruction with that of the Upaniṣads and Śaṅkara. For this purpose, there is no need to discuss in detail Derrida's obscure and arcane writings.

Suffice it to clearly state his concept of deconstruction and compare it with that of the Upaniṣads and Śaṅkara, as has been clarified above. According to Derrida, logocentric traditions are those which display biases toward speech and Being and against writing and Becoming. Several systems of Western philosophy and the Upanisadic tradition are regarded by Derrida as exemplars of logocentrism. However, according to Derrida, logocentrism is itself a direct consequence of a fundamental error, namely, that of elevating one member of a pair of opposites over the other. Thus in the pairs being and becoming, identity and difference, good and evil, self and other, male and female, the first member of each of the pairs is given a privileged and exalted status and the second is regarded as a corruption of the first. In this manner, not only systems of philosophy in which being is elevated over becoming but also those in which the reverse is the case — becoming is exalted over being (Heraclitus and certain versions of Buddhism) — are guilty of the error of preferring and bestowing privileged status on one of the elements of a pair of opposites over the other. Deconstruction, then, is the process of recognizing this error of exalting and elevating one member of a pair of opposites over the other, the correcting of the error, and eventually commanding constant vigilance against committing such error. Thus Derrida and Śaṅkara seem to agree on the point that the conceptual oppositions, which are the warp and woof of language, are the obstacles to our experience of the real. Only by overcoming these obstacles — the trap of language — do we experience the real. But Derrida and Sankara seriously disagree on the way to overcome these obstacles. For the Upaniṣads and Śaṅkara, the way is through total, full and complete transcendence of language. In contrast, for Derrida, "... this trap may be escaped by staying within language but on the middle path between the opposites. When the opposites of language are maintained in dynamic tension through a continual deconstruction of first one opposite and then the other, the real is experienced. For the moment the real is spoken it is tending to swing the pendulum towards either one or the other of the opposites. Only by a continual deconstruction and reversing of each pendulum swing may we experience the real as the middle point — where the tension between the pairs is momentarily in balance . . . such a process of continual deconstructing, with its ongoing need for deconstruction, is itself the real."[1] Further, for Derrida, there is nothing outside the text; there is no experience outside of language; there can be no experience in which language is wholly absent. Thus, "Whereas Derrida's discriminative deconstruction constantly goes on as the very essence of reality, for Śaṅkara, after the *anubhava* or direct intuition of *Brahman*, no reflective consideration is possible for there is no language or thought-content left to reflect upon. Whereas for Derrida there is nothing outside of language or text, for Sankara there is nothing of the text left in the *anubhava* experience. The text is the subject that the Upaniṣadic '*neti, neti*' cancels out to enable the real to be known."[2] It should be clear from the above quotes that Derrida's deconstruction is not the same as the Upaniṣadic (Śaṅkara's) desuperimposition. Yes, desuperimposition is surely deconstruction, a thorough disassembling, with absolutely no remainder in which to emphasize one concept over another. But Derrida's deconstruction is still fully within superimposition. Thus we note that desuperimposition is sufficient condition for deconstruction but not *vice-versa*.

Thus both Śaṅkara and Derrida realize that the trap of language has to be overcome, and Śaṅkara's way of overcoming is through total transcendence of language, whereas Derrida's is through engagement in continual deconstructing. For Śaṅkara, there is the non-dual reality (*Brahman*) of which the text speaks, and the purpose of the text is not to inform and describe but to inspire and motivate one to the quest for *Brahman*. But it is

---

1. Harold Coward, *Derrida and Indian Philosophy* (State University of New York Press, Albany, New York), 1990, pp. 88-89.

2. *Ibid.*, p. 97.

difficult to see how Derrida's continual deconstruction is equatable to experience of the real and self-realization: "Both Śaṅkara and Derrida have a practical goal in mind in their philosophy of language. For them, the philosophy of language is not just abstract theorizing; it has the practical goal of spiritual self-realization. Between them, however, the nature of this self-realization is quite different: for Śaṅkara it requires the total transcending of language, whereas for Derrida it is found in the prophetic call for action that comes to us from the very midst of language itself'."[3] This quote makes explicit reference to spiritual self-realization. I have no wish to engage here in a discussion of prophetic calls for action. I shall content myself with a brief discussion of what I construe to be the main point of disagreement between Śaṅkara and Derrida. But let me first make the following remarks. In the light of our earlier discussion of the Upaniṣadic teaching and Śaṅkara, is it in the first place appropriate to compare Saṅkara and Derrida? Yes, one can appropriately compare them as philosophers; but one should not forget that Śaṅkara is primarily a spiritual teacher; philosophy for him is not constructing and advancing pictures of reality; rather, it is an instrument, only an instrument, *albeit* defective and inadequate, for revealing *Brahman*; but, used skilfully, it can awaken one to the quest for *Brahman*. It is worth mentioning here that for Śaṅkara language as Veda is the sole means for the realization of *Brahman*. But in the end, in the *anubhava*, even the Vedas and the *mahāvākyas* are to be transcended, in full accord with the spirit of the teaching of the *Muṇḍaka Upaniṣad*.

The Upaniṣadic and Śaṅkara's way to the experience of reality is through total transcendence of language and thought, where there is neither identity nor difference. Consequently, it is a serious error to say that reality for the Upaniṣadic teachers is substance or that Śaṅkara is a substance-philosopher.

Now to the point of disagreement. This disagreement at once

3. *Ibid.*, p. 91

brings into clear focus a fundamental difference between the Western and Upaniṣadic traditions. It is this: Is there or is there not a mode of being wholly outside of language? The Upanisads and Śaṅkara maintain that there is indeed such a mode of being, whereas the Western philosopher maintains that there is no such mode and there, can in principle, be no such mode. We can reformulate the above question as follows: Is there or is there not a state of consciousness without objects — objectless consciousness? Once again the Upanisạds and Saṅkara affirm and Western philosophers, including the phenomenologists, deny such a state. The reason for this difference is to be sought in the different ways in which 'mind'(*manas*) is understood in the Upanisadic and Western traditions. For the Upanisads, mind is a phenomenon, a subtle sense-organ, and like all other phenomena mind arises and passes away. Being a phenomenon, mind is also an object of consciousness. For this reason, the terms, 'mind', 'I', 'self', and 'consciousness' are not synonymous; further, consciousness is *not* a phenomenon, and hence one can never, in principle, experience consciousness as one alongside other objects. In short, consciousness is transcendental 'Transcendental' here is not to be understood as beyond our ken and pale; rather, it means 'cannot be experienced as a *phenomenon*'. In clear contrast, in the Western tradition, the terms listed above are used synonymously. Thus remember Descartes' ruminations: "What then is it that I am? A thinking thing . . .What now shall I say of the mind itself, i.e. of myself? . . . For it might indeed be that if I entirely ceased to think, I should thereupon altogether cease to exist . . . I am therefore only a thinking thing, a *mind*, an understanding or reason."[4] Thus for Descartes and the Western tradition in general 'I', 'mind', 'self', and 'consciousness' are synonymous. Accordingly, in the Western tradition, it is held that there cannot, in principle, be objectless state of consciousness. But Śaṅkara and the Upanisadic seers

4. *Meditation* II.

would like to ask Descartes and the Western philosophers in general how they know that one altogether ceases to exist when one ceases to think. The point here is that for the Western philosopher thinking never ceases and for the Upaniṣads there surely is a mode of being devoid of language and thought. Derrida shares this Western view: "Again we are reminded of Mādhyamika and the relentless critic of the *catuṣkoṭi* as the basic task of philosophy. Derrida would agree, but he would deny the Buddhist and Advaita contention that another option is open; namely the transcending of the trap of language altogether. For Derrida there is no *anubhava* or *śūnya* experience of the real outside of language. At this point Derrida is a typical Western philosopher in his view that it is in the midst of the existential struggle, not beyond it, that the real is most fully realized."[5] I am not at all interested in a claim's being typically Western or non-Western; my concern is with rational grounds (or lack thereof) for any claim. How does Derrida know that there is no *anubhava*, experience of reality transcending language and thought? Are we to accept his claim without demanding clarification and grounds? For my part, I cannot. The heart of the matter here is that the question whether or not there is an objectless state of being cannot be answered by appeals to dogma and tradition or by fiat of definition. This question is a fundamental phenomenological question and can only be answered by phenomenological investigation. Such investigation is singularly lacking in Derrida and the Western tradition in general. This is not the place to go into this question in any detail. All that needs to be said is that a careful reading and analysis of the *Māṇḍūkya Upaniṣad* is the most fruitful starting point in one's efforts to answer this question. I shall now make a few pertinent remarks. In the state of deep sleep, one is conscious of neither external objects nor internal objects; that is, mind is not functioning during deep sleep. This in turn means that our experience of *objects*, external

5. Coward, *op. cit.*, p. 89.

as well as internal, is due to the activity of mind. Further, although during deep sleep one is not aware that one is in deep sleep, nevertheless, when one wakes up one reports that one has had a deep, sound, and enjoyable sleep. This means that one is conscious that one has been unconscious (of objects). This is not possible unless consciousness exists in the state of deep sleep. Such a state of consciousness is indeed the state of objectless consciousness. The Upaniṣads may be mistaken in this conclusion, but they attempt to support it by phenomenological considerations, unlike Derrida, who offers nothing more than the flat and dogmatic assertion that there can be no experience outside of language. I am truly amazed that Coward thinks that by this wholly unsupported denial Derrida presents a serious challenge to Śaṅkara and the Upaniṣads: " . . . Derrida would surely challenge Śaṅkara's notion of *anubhava* as a pure perception free of the *avidyā* of language. Because Derrida does not believe that anything like 'pure perception' — that is, perception free of representation or interpretation — exists, his challenge to Śaṅkara is significant."[6] First, I am not interested in what Derrida believes or does not believe; I am only interested in his reasons, if any, for a belief he holds. Obviously, Derrida does not offer any reasons for his belief that there cannot be anything like Śaṅkara's *anubhava*, but merely proclaims his belief, and it is difficult to see how Derrida's mere proclamation of his wholly unsupported belief constitutes a *significant* challenge to Śaṁkara. In my judgement, such an empty proclamation of belief is not a challenge at all, let alone the question whether it is significant. Second, talk of perception, whether pure or impure, is wholly inappropriate and positively misleading when discussing Śaṅkara'*anubhava*; for the *anubhava* Śaṅkara speaks of is neither perception nor non-perception. Śaṁkara and the Upaniṣadic seers never talk of *anubhava* as a perception of any kind whatever. Perception is always of phenomena — objects. In

6. *Ibid.*, p. 98.

the *anubhava* of Saṅkara, one does not *perceive Brahman*, the non-dual reality, as something opposed to and different from the perceiver. As the Upanisads consistently teach, in the *anubhava*, one becomes *Brahman*, for here with the cessation of mind the tripartite distinction of knower, known, and the act of knowing, characteristic of all ordinary (dualistic) knowing — perception — is itself transcended. Thus Derrida's continual deconstruction to overcome the trap of language (difference) never leaves the domain of superimposition and consequently of *Saguṇa-Brahman*.

It is well-known that according to the Sāṁkhya there are two ultimates, *prakṛti* and *purusa*. *Prakṛti* is the world of phenomena. It is to be emphasized that it is misleading to translate '*prakrti*', as many do, as the physical (material) world. For *prakrti* is not just the material world, but all timebound existence, which includes thoughts and emotions. *Puruṣa* is pure consciousness, the so-called self of the Sāṁkhya. And Sāṁkhya maintains that *prakrti* and *purusa* are radically different from each other, and thereby encounters the serious problem of accounting for the observed relation between the two — a problem akin to the Cartesian mind-body problem. The question here is: how can any relation obtain between *prakrti* and *purusa*, claimed to be so radically — absolutely — different from each other? In particular, the Sāṁkhya has to explain how the *puruṣa*, so different from *prakrti*, can initiate the latter's evolution. The Sāṁkhya has no satisfactory and acceptable answers to these questions.

Advaita-Vedānta rejects as absurd and untenable the Sāṁkhya thesis of two ultimates, but finds acceptable its theory of evolution of *prakṛti*, with certain modifications. The general Advaita-Vedānta view concerning the world of phenomena is as follows: Reality (*Brahman*) does not undergo any *real* changes, since all changes are changes in appearances — forms and names — only. And since *Brahman* is the ultimate, non-dual reality, the evolution of the worlds of phenomena as well as their dissolution into the primordial, formless and nameless reality is due to *Brahman* Itself. and not due to some external cause. Consistent with this view, Śaṅkara upholds the *satkāryavāda* version of causation. *Satkaryavada* is the doctrine that the effect pre-exists in the cause. Thus everything in the world of phenomena exists as potentiality in (of) *Brahman* — has its foundation in *Brahman*. In short, *Brahman* is the material, formal, efficient, and final cause of the world of phenomena.

In contemporary cosmology, there is considerable evidence for the Big Bang theory, according to which the whole universe and countless objects therein came to be as a result of the explosion of a primordial black hole — a singularity. Prior to the Big Bang, there was neither space nor time nor matter nor any other *manifestation* of energy. This means that space, time, matter, and all phenomena were 'created' by the Big Bang itself, It further means that the primordial black hole itself was non-spatial and non-temporal, and all our familiar conceptions of space, time, and matter break down with regard to the black hole itself. Precisely this characterization applies to the *Brahman* of Advaita-Vedānta.

Thus the Big Bang theory of modern cosmology is in full harmony with the Advaita-Vedānta teaching of the periodic evolutions and dissolutions of the worlds of phenomena. Further, Advaita-Vedānta and the Indian tradition in general, unlike almost all other traditions, had long been familiar with concepts of vast scales of space and time; for this reason, the modern cosmological estimate of the age of the universe — the time since the last Big Bang — as approximately 15-18 billion years is neither shocking nor blasphemous to Advaita-Vedānta. It might also be of interest to note here that Darwin's theory of evolution, which continues to be a subject of fierce controversy and heated debate in the West, on account of its allegedly sacrilegious teachings, is in perfect accord with the vision of Advaita-Vedānta. Advaita-Vedāntins may even correctly say that Darwin went quite far but not far enough, for he only taught the essential unity of all life-forms and not the essential unity of all existence, which is at the very heart of Advaita-Vedānta. Yes, Advaita-Vedānta is radical and thoroughgoing reductionism and not the half-baked and absurd reductionism widespread in the West. Why is the Western conception of reductionism half-baked and absurd? The reason is that its aim is to reduce all kinds of *phenomena*, without residuum, to one particular kind of phenomena, namely, the so-called physical (material). What the Western reductionist fails to ask is: the physical, the mental, the emotional are all equally given to me as phenomena; if so, on what grounds am I entitled to think and claim that some particular kind of phenomena is ontologically more fundamental than other kinds of phenomena (and to which they are all to be reduced)? No Western reductionist ever gave me an acceptable answer to this question. Let me emphatically state that this kind of reductionism cannot, in principle, succeed. Sane and sensible reductionistic programs should aim at establishing correlations among different kinds of phenomena, for example between the mental and the neurophysiological. But correlation is not the same as identity, for identity cannot be attained at the phenomenal level, the world of phenomena. In keen contrast, the Advaita-Vedāntic reductionism reduces all varieties of phenomena to *Brahman*, which is not Itself a phenomenon; and that is how it should be, according to the highest standards of rationality. I cannot sensibly ask: What is *Brahman* made of? But I can sensibly ask this question of *any* phenomenon, which is understood as anything that is (or can, in principle, be) an *object* of consciousness. *Brahman* is not any one particular kind of *thing* (*entity*); for if It were, It could not at once be all entities, actual and potential. Thus the reductionism of Advaita-Vedānta is not empirical reductionism but rather the reduction of all phenomena to transcendental *Brahman*. A more correct way to convey this point is as follows: it is not that all phenomena are reducible (reduced) to *Brahman*, but their very being is always the transcendental *Brahman*. This realization is precisely what is signalled by the *mahavakya*, 'all this is *Brahman*, whatever exists is *Brahman*, nothing other than *Brahman* exists'.

Advaita-Vedānta rejects as absurd the Sāṁkhya claim of two ultimates, namely, *puruṣa* and *prakṛti*. It is absurd because the Sāṁkhya, while maintaining on the one hand that these two are radically different from each other, nevertheless appeals on the other hand to the *puruṣa* to initiate the evolution of the allegedly wholly unconscious *prakṛti*. In vivid contrast, Advaita-Vedānta upholds the Upanisadic teaching of thoroughgoing non-dualism: ultimate reality is the non-dual *Brahman*, which is none other than *atman*, pure, objectless consciousness. Since *Brahman* is the sole reality, there can be nothing other than *Brahman* to trigger the manifestation of *Brahman*. Put directly, *Brahman*, the ultimate non-dual reality, is self-contained and triggers Its own manifestation. It is remarkable that current researches in cosmology are guided by the idea of a self-contained, self-triggering, non-dual reality and not by the Sāṁkhya idea of two ultimates. Theories aimed at establishing such a non-dual reality are known as 'theories of supersymmetry and supergravity' (with spontaneous quantum fluctuations).

I come now to the Einstein-Podolsky-Rosen paradox. It is well-known that Heisenberg's uncertainty principle, also called the 'indeterminacy principle', is a fundamental theorem governing the whole of quantum theory. There are many logically equivalent variations of this principle, the most comprehensive and significant of these being known as 'Bohr's principle of complementarity'. According to this principle, microphysical reality has no determinate nature prior to our experimental investigation; rather, the nature of microphysical reality depends upon the kind of experiment the inquirer chooses to set up. To illustrate, if someone claims that electrons are particles, I can set up an experiment which reveals the presence of the electron as a wave and not as a particle. The reason for this is that an experimental set-up in which the electron is detected as a wave destroys all the claimed particle properties, and vice versa. This is to say that it is in principle impossible to detect in a single experimental set-up both particle and wave properties. This observation has far-reaching consequences. Reality does not in itself have any determinate structure or form, prior to and independently of our experimentation; rather, it is in the power of the experimenter to make reality manifest itself as a particle or a wave, depending upon his choice, whim, and fancy. All of this is in stark contrast to the situation in classical — Newtonian, pre-quantam — physics, where it was believed as an axiom that reality in itself has a determinate structure. To say that how reality manifests itself to an inquirer depends upon his or her choice of experimental set-up, is to say that claims concerning the nature of reality depend upon the superimpositional — adhyāsaic — framework of the inquirer, 'superimpositional framework' being understood as including not just the experimental equipment but also the investigator's psycho-physiological constitution — perceptual-conceptual makeup — and thereby his theories. What better testimony can one offer on behalf of the Advaita-Vedānta principle of superimposition (*adhyāsa*)? Reality, *Brahman*, in Itself has no nature or form or structure; only appearances of reality can have natures, forms, and structures, and appearances are always in relation to a perceiver, an inquirer, a locus of consciousness.

Einstein refused to accept Bohr's principle of complementarity and its consequences (described above) and doggedly adhered to a deterministic thesis. Remember his declaration that God does not play dice with the world. But progress in physics increasingly confirms the contrary, that God *does* play dice with the world; it seems that He (She?) not only plays dice with the world but immensely delights and enjoys doing so. Remember our *purāṇas* which narrate wonderful stories of Śiva's playing dice with his consort Śakti and sometimes even losing because She cheats! In 1935 Einstein and two of his colleagues, Podolsky and Rosen, published a paper (hereafter referred to as 'the EPR paper') to show that quantum mechanical description of reality is incomplete and hence flawed. The strategy of this paper consists of showing, within the framework of the principles and rules of quantum theory, that, contrary to the uncertainty principle, a microphysical entity must have both a position and a momentum, before any prediction is made and hence before a choice is made by an experimenter as to which of these variables to measure. The EPR paper thus aimed at demonstrating a contradiction in the quantum theroy. It follows that experimental confirmation of the central claim of the EPR paper will show the quantum theory to be inconsistent and therefore its description of reality incomplete and false.

The EPR paper was discussed by physicists and philosophers for over four decades, before it could be put to experimental test. And with the publication of Bell's theorem, it became possible to experimentally test the conclusions of the EPR paper. The experiment showed that there is, contrary to the EPR thesis and the special theory of relativity, instantaneous transmission of information between two regions of the world, no matter how far apart, without the passing of any signals between the regions. Such transmission of information can only be due to signals travelling faster than light, in clear contradiction to the postulate of the special theory of relativity, namely, the velocity of light in empty space is the maximum velocity attainable by any signal.

Instantaneous transmission of information between widely separated regions of the world has grave consequences to the traditional and entrenched concept of causality. Thus consider two events, say *P* and *Q*, which are simultaneous. Assume that the signal from one event to the other is a tachyon (a hypothetical particle travelling faster than light). Now, for an observer from a different frame of reference, *P* could be the cause of *Q*. However, since the order of events could also be observed in the reverse, for another observer *Q* would appear as the cause of *P*. What all this means, then, is that simultaneously happening events in different locations can be observed as happening in opposite time-orders. It is clear that such events could not be causally connected. Where does all this leave us? If the quantum theory is a complete theory of reality, there must exist some special kind of connection between events widely separated in the space-time continuum. Such a connection is referred to as 'non-local causality', a baffling and mysterious concept indeed.

But since all parts of the universe are connected with each other during the Big Bang, non-local causation and hence instantaneous communication exist among all parts of the cosmos. And this observation is fully consistent with the teaching of Advaita-Vedānta that all phenomena (appearances), being founded in *Brahman*, the non-dual reality, are connected with each other. Indeed, at the level of *Brahman*, they are not different phenomena but rather are one and the same non-dual reality, and hence instantaneous communication. The world, therefore, is not an Aristotelian world of isolated substances with external relations but rather is a world of interdependent phenomena. In short, the world is weblike, holistic, and organismic and not atomistic.

John Clauser, among the physicists to first experimentally test Bell's theorem, remarked that the refutation of the EPR thesis and hence of local causality in quantum mechanics is at once the refutation of the much cherished view of the world of objectivity and locality. According to the principle of two kinds of knowledge and truth, which is a central teaching of the Upaniṣads and Advaita-Vedānta, all rational-scientific truths are relative truths. But 'relative truth' does not mean falsehood; rather, it means truth certifiable by all inquirers who are constituted alike and conduct their inquiry with a certain categorial framework. In this sense, the truths of science, including those of contemporary physics, are *objective* truths. However, 'objective truth' does not mean *absolute* truth, in the sense of truth that has nothing whatever to do with any and all inquirers. Thus, Advaita-

Vedānta, along with contemporary physics, acknowldedges objective truths and the conception (view) of the world to which these truths belong and apply, and rejects as dogmatic and absurd any suggestion that the world in itself, independently of all inquirers — beings — is thus-and-such. The inquirer — consciousness — is the very pivot of the enterprise of categorial knowledge and cannot be dispensed with.

The famous (or notorious) case of Schrödinger's cat also points to the indispensability of the observer — consciousness. Imagine a cat placed in a box equipped with a triggering mechanism which can be activated by the decay of a radioactive atom, provided the emitted particle strikes a photocell. On the activation of the trigger, poisonous gas will be released into the box. If the emitted particle does not strike the photocell, the trigger will not be activated and no poisonous gas will be released into the box. Assume that the half life of the readioactive atom is two hours. Now since radioactive decay is genuinely statistical and random, it cannot be predicted with any certainty; and after two hours of placing the cat in the box, the entire system is described by the quantum theory as one of the superimpositions of two states, one in which the cat is alive and the other in which the cat is dead. As far as the quantum theory is concerned, it is impossible to predict with any certainty whether the cat will be alive or dead. However, on opening the box, the observer finds the cat in one or the other of the two states. The question here is: does this mean that the observer's opening the box and looking into it collapsed the wavepacket — wavefunction — thereby throwing the system into a definite state? According to Bohr and Heisenberg, the answer is clearly in the affirmative; that the quantum theory cannot predict with certainty the state of the cat does not mean that the theory is incomplete; rather, it only points to the essential role of the observer. There can be no talk of the state (nature) of reality apart from the observer. There is simply no way of dispensing with the observer (consciousness). Consciousness inevitably enters into quantum mechanical consideration of reality, the reason for this being the indivisibility of Planck's quantum of action (h), which is none other than the indivisibility of the observer and the system being observed. Put pointedly, the observer and the observed form an indivisible whole.

There are many interpretations of the Schrödinger-cat puzzle. I have neither the wish nor the time to go here into the details of the so-called parallel-universes interpretation, and shall only make a few pertinent observations. According to this interpretation, the observer does not collapse the wavepacket and thereby throw the system into a definite state; rather, there exist simultaneously a number of universes in each of which the system is in one of the possible states. Thus Schrödinger's cat exists simultaneously in two universes, one in which it is alive and the other in which it is dead. Further, an observer in a given universe will be aware of only his universe and not others, and one cannot move sideward, as it were, from one universe to another. But, one would like to ask, on what grounds should one accept the claim that parallel universes exist? Is there any evidence? None, to the best of my knowledge and belief; and I leave it for the readers to judge the scientific character (or lack thereof) of an interpretation which claims the simultaneous existence of countless parallel universes, none of which except one's own, can, in principle, be observed. It is also to be noted that the very concept of parallel *universes* is amusingly absurd; for, if by 'universe' one means the totality of existence, actual and possible, how can one talk of many universes? Perhaps 'parallel worlds' is the appropriate phrase and concept. But somehow the absurd phrase 'parallel universes' gained currency and great staying power, just as, because of Columbus' erroneous beliefs, native Americans continue to be referred to as 'Indians'.

It is my considered judgement that Bohr's is the most rational and least magical of all the attempts thus far to resolve the Schrödinger-cat paradox. Let me now briefly consider the main objections of its opponents. It has been claimed by some that

Bohr s interpretation and resolution logically lead to solipsism, a position which on the one hand is regarded as logically irrefutable while condemned on the other as absurd and untenable. Yes, solipsism should certainly seem absurd and untenable to those whose conceptions of objectivity and objective truth are themselves unquestionably absurd and irrational. In other words, solipsism is objectionable and unpalatable only to those who are ignorant of the Upanisadic teaching of two kinds of truth and knowledge. But solipsism makes good sense in the light of this teaching. If *Brahman* — ultimate non-dual reality — is non-different from *ātman*, pure, objectless consciousness, the Self of all beings, then it is correct to say that only the Self (*ātman*) is and nothing else. Thus solipsism is not a lower truth (*vyāvahārika satya*) but the higher truth (*paramarthika satya*). But if in ignorance one mistakes the higher truth for a lower truth, then confusion and magical solutions are but inevitable, along with bad metaphysics. I therefore conclude that Bohr's resolution of the cat-paradox is in full harmony with the higher truth taught by the Upaniṣads and Advaita-Vedānta, through the principle of two kinds of knowledge and truth. Let me remind, then, that solipsism is not an empirical but transcendental thesis. It is most appropriate here to quote John Wheeler, a distinguished contemporary physicist: Starting from the Big Bang, the universe expands and cools; after thousands of millions of years it produces beings capable of observing the universe, and "acts of observer-participicancy — via the mechanism of the delayed — 'reality' to the universe not only now but back to the beginning".

I shall now briefly deal with the quest for elementary particles, the so-called basic building blocks of the universe. The search for basic building blocks is an ancient quest. Beginning with Ionian and Indian speculations, later revived by Dalton, the quest continues in our own day with ever-growing list of elementary particles. Where and when does the quest end? Do we have any good reasons to think that, given enough time, we will one day hit upon the ultimate building blocks? The answer, according to Advaita-Vedānta, is clearly in the nagative, and is a direct consequence of its central teachings. No, the search can never, in participle, end, as long as it is conducted through categorial frameworks. And, let us note, apart from some framework or other, there can be no such search at all. Since every phenomenon is an appearance and hence sublatable by other phenomena, no phenomenon can be thought of as *ultimate*, and no judgement about it can be regarded as absolute truth, descriptive of ultimate reality (*Brahman*). And since every phenomenon is necessarily a dependent existent, one inevitably asks: if *X*, *Y*, and *Z* are the ultimate building blocks, what are the relations among *X*, *Y*, and *Z*? Thus think of quarks, you will see the point. The point here is that where there is plurality there can be no talk of ultimacy. This is precisely what is meant by saying that the domain of phenomena — the world of phenomena — is one of relations and vice versa. Ultimate reality, *Brahman*, is not a domain of plurality and it is therefore absurd to talk about any relations with regard to It. This is to say that *Brahman* is *not* an *entity*, for to be an entity is to be a dependent existent and therefore a composite and not ultimate; nor can *Brahman* be related to anything, for there cannot, in principle, be anything beside *Brahman*. One cannot even claim that a particular kind of particles, say Funnions, are the ultimate building blocks; for such a claim implies that Funnions constitute ultimate reality, and this makes ultimate reality a composite being — a contradiction — unlike *Brahman*, non-dual, impartite, and unitary.

Is it not true that from time to time we are informed that the ultimate particle has been captured? And is it not also true that not long after such a proclamation we are told that the latest investigation has shown that the particle (mistakenly) believed to be ultimate was really constituted of other particles, say, Elusons? It should be clear by now that, according to Advaita-Vedānta, the quest for basic — ultimate — building blocks is an unending quest. But this is no reason for lament and despair. On the contrary, the ever-expanding frontiers of rational-scientific — perceptual-conceptual — knowledge, through the construction of categorial frameworks, are glowing testimony to the creativity of the human spirit as well as of reality, implied by the claim of its incapturability in any framework. All this is in perfect accord with our understanding that there can be no room in rational-scientific inquiries for any absolute claims — claims descriptive of ultimate reality. Our categorial frameworks make us keenly aware of the untold complexity of the enterprise of knowledge they require us to launch upon, thereby enabling us to appreciate the inexhaustible richness and variety of the manifestations of reality and marvel at and celebrate the power and fecundity of human imagination. Yes, Advaita-Vedānta would say, the deeper we penetrate into what we call 'things, objects', the more we see of ourselves in them; they impress us as evanescent energy-patterns, which ubiquitously appear, disappear, and reappear (even in a vacuum) and are identified and related to each other through some categorial framework (of ours, and not of some other beings). '*Māyā*', in one of its meanings, connotes this extraordinarily subtle, incredibly complex, and irresolvably paradoxical panorama of appearances, characterized by unceasing dynamism.

I cannot go here into a detailed discussion of the currently fashionable topic of Theories of Everything. I shall content myself with making a few remarks. A theory of everything has to explain how the universe came about and show that this universe is unique. Gödel's incompleteness theorem and the difficulties associated with specifying the cosmic initial conditions present insuperable objections against the possibility of such a theory. Further, the Advaita-Vedāntin will ask: if the theory of everything accounts for everything, what accounts for the theory? Put differently, nothing from within the universe can account for the arising of the universe. Looking for a theory of everything is no more and no less than looking for an answer to the question: why did the non-dual *Brahman* become many? This question itself betrays *avidyā*, for it presupposes that something — an event —

happened to *Brahman* and consequently It became many. *Brahman* is timeless and without a second, and hence not subject to events and happenings (which belong in and pertain to phenomena, timebound existence). Thus there can be nothing within the world of phenomena by which to answer the above (misleading) question. Hence Advaita-Vedānta teaches that the existence of the world is *anirvacanīya*, indefinable and inexplicable. But this is no reason for lament; for when one understands *Brahman* as non-dual and transcendental, one sees the absurdity of asking the question as well as attempting to answer it. The proper question to ask is: why does the non-dual *Brahman appear* to us as many. Note that this question does not commit the errors underlying the other question.

To conclude: (1) The Upaniṣadic seers and Śaṅkara are primarily spiritual teachers (*gurus*) and not mere philosophers and scholars (*pandits*); accordingly, their chief concern is with inspiring and motivating the listener to seek reality, *Brahman*, *ātman*, the true self, enlightenment. (2) This does not, however, mean that there are no philosophical concepts and observations in the Upaniṣads or that Śaṅkara is not a philosopher. Quite to the contrary, Śaṅkara's Vedanta is a system of original and profound philosophic thought. (3) The main purpose of employment of philosophical concepts and arguments in the Upaniṣads and Śankara is not to construct and advance theories and pictures of reality, but to inspire and motivate the listener to the quest for reality, *Brahman*. Hence *adhyaropa-apavāda* (desuperimposition): concepts are forged and arguments advanced and in the end rescinded, thereby warning the listener not to *literally* understand either the premises or the conclusions of the arguments, lest the listener be misled and trapped in puzzles and paradoxes and thereby lose sight of the fundamental goal, namely, the experience of reality. (4) Language is used in the Upanisads and Śaṅkara primarily non-conceptually (non-referentially), as different from conceptual and referential use in the pursuit of categorial truths (perceptual-conceptual truths) which is *vyavaharika satya.* Language is like the finger pointing to the moon and the raft used for crossing a stream, which are to be abandoned after they have served their purposes. It is worth mentioning here that the Zen Master's use of koans is exemplary of non-conceptual use of language (and this is not accidental). (5) Upanisadic and Śaṅkara's desuperimposition, unlike Derrida's deconstruction, is *radical* deconstruction, leaving at the end only the experience of reality and absolutely no pairs of opposites between which to engage in continual deconstruction. (6) Therefore, Upanisadic desuperimposition is sufficient condition for thorough and radical deconstruction, and Derrida's deconstruction, in so far as it still lies within superimposition, is not sufficient condition for Upaniṣadic desuperimposition. (7) Derrida's claim that there is nothing outside of language cannot even be consistently stated; for how is one to know whether or not there is anything at all outside of language? If, on Derrida's own admission, he cannot get out of language, what entitles him to say whether or not there is anything outside of language? It is like someone who cannot get outside of the room he is in saying that there is nothing outside of the room (this is an analogy, not an argument). To be able to correctly claim that there is nothing outside of language, one has to get outside of lang0e of language is not a claim about language; rather, it is about whether there is anything outside of language. In sharp contrast, the Upaniṣads and Śaṅkara consistently maintain that only by getting outside of language can one know whether there is anything outside of language, and they answer that there is indeed the non-dual reality, which is at once objectless consciousness. It is appropriate to emphasize here that mystics in other times and climes, for example Meister Eckhart and Al Halaj, also agree with the Upaniṣads and reject Derrida's claim that there is nothing outside of language. (8) Derrida does not seem to realize that his talk of hearing the prophetic call for ethical action is a product of superimposition — *vikalpa* — and exaltation of stories from a particular tradition to an absolute status. (9) Traditions in which mysticism is central are at once traditions of radical deconstruction, the desuperimposition the Upaniṣads untiringly teach. (10) There is nothing new about Derrida's deconstructionism, for, as we have shown, full, complete, and thoroughgoing deconstructionism — radical deconstructionism — is as old as the Upaniṣadic tradition itself. (11) It is no exaggeration to say that no other tradition is so profoundly struck as Advaita-Vedānta by the fact that we are conscious beings. That we are conscious beings is a stupendous mystery, a mystery far greater than the existence of the universe itself. For this reason, consciousness had come to occupy the central place in the vision of Advaita-Vedānta. And we have seen that consciousness has entered into contemporary physics through the quantum theory. This should be no surprise, for is it not true that consciousness, so near and yet so far, is the fulcrum on which turns all talk of the universe and truth, relative or absolute? (12) Let there be no misunderstanding here. We are keenly aware that all rational-scientific truths are categorial (lower) truths, and are therefore tentative and subject to revision, modification, and even outright rejection (sublation in general). In other words, there can be no room for finality and absolute truth in the rational-scientific enterprise. Thus what I have attempted to show in this lecture is not that modern physics *confirms* Advaita-Vedānta but rather that modern physics is in full harmony with the vision of Advaita-Vedānta. We should always bear in mind the following questions: when one discusses science and religion, is it the aim of the discussion to show that science supports one's religion or one's religion supports science? It is the pinnacle of *avidyā* to try to support one's religion by science, as it is to try to support science by one's religion. Science does not need the support of religion and religion does not need the support of science. Let me emphasize here that Advaita-Vedānta is not a religion in the usual sense, with God, the Sultan in the sky, and his necessary adversary, the Devil, and heavens and hells. Advaita-Vedānta is the quest for the *paramārtha* and hence does not contradict science and rationality. And, what is more,

Advaita-Vedānta points to the *paramartha* through rational considerations: that is, rationality is made full use of in pointing to the higher truth. For this reason, Advaita-Vedānta is not a foe of science and rationality; quite to the contrary, through its own commitment to the highest standards of rationality and fidelity of experience, it will always be in natural harmony and accord with the best of all rational pursuits, including science.

To say that a body of knowledge, say *X*, is in harmony with another body of knowledge, say *Y*, is not to say that the propositions making up *X* are necessarily found in *Y* (or vice versa), either implicitly or explicitly; rather, it is to say that there is no proposition in *X* that contradicts any proposition in *Y* and there is no proposition in *Y* that contradicts any proposition in *X*; put pointedly, the propositions of *X* and *Y* constitute a consistent set of propositions. This point is best appreciated through a contrasting illustration. See how Western religious fundamentalists oppose modern science with their Biblical doctrine of Creationism, by regarding the latter as a competing scientific theory (proposition). And when I say that Advaita-Vedānta is in full harmony and accord with modern science, I mean that there is here no room for such conflicts and oppositions. I humbly submit that such conflicts are but a natural consequence of the conspicuous lack in a tradition of the teaching of two kinds of knowledge and truth.

Selected Bibliography

Alain Aspect, Jean Dalibard, Gerard Roger, "Experimental Test of Bell's Inequalities Using Time-varying Analyzers", *Physical Review*, Letters 49, 1804, 1982.

John D. Barrow, *The World within the World*, Oxford University Press, 1988.

——, *Theories of Everything: The Quest for Ultimate Explanation*, Oxford University Press, New York, 1991.

John S. Bell, "On the Einstein-Podolsky-Rosen Paradox", *Physics*, 1, 195, 1964.

Richard Boyd, Philip Gasper, and J.D. Trout, *The Philosophy of Science*, The MIT Press, Cambridge, MA, 1992.

J. Clauser and M. Horne, "Experimental Consequences of Objective Local Theories", *Physical Review*, D 10, 532, 1974.

Harold Coward, *Derrida and Indian Philosophy*, State University of New York Press, Albany, NY, 1990.

Bernard d' Espagnat, *Conceptual Foundations of Quantum Mechanics* (second edition), W.A. Benjamin, Reading, MA, 1976.

Albert Einstein, Boris Podolsky, Nathan Rosen, "Can Quantum Mechanical Description of Physical Reality be Considered Complete?" *Physical Review*, 47, 777, 1935.

Swami Gambhirananda, (tr.), *Eight Upanishads: With the Commentary of Sankaracarya*, Vols. I & II, Advaita Ashrama, Calcutta, 1957; and *Brahma-Sutra Bhasya of Sankaracarya*, Advaita Ashrama, Calcutta, 1965.

John Gribbin, *In Search of Schrodinger's Cat; Quantum Physics and Reality*, Bantam Books, New York, 1984.

John Horgan, *The End of Science*, Helix Books, Reading, MA, 1996.

Kenneth K. Inada, (tr.) *Nagarjuna: A Translation of His Mulamadhyamakārikā, with an Introductory Essay*, The Hokuseido Press, Tokyo, 1970.

Max Jammer, *The Philosophy of Quantum Mechanics*, Wiley, NY, 1974.

Thomas S. Kuhn, *The Structure of Scientific Revolutions* (second edition, enlarged), The University of Chicago Press, Chicago, 1970.

David Lindley, *The End of Physics: The Myth of a Unified Theory*, Basic Books, NY, 1993.

Swami Nikhilananda (tr.), *The Upanishads*, four volumes, Advaita Ashrama, Calcutta.

Ramakrishna Puligandla, *Jnana-Yoga (The Way Of Knowledge): An Analytical Interpretation*; New Delhi, D.K. Printworld, Indian edition, 1997.